I Can't
Believe I'm Not
Bitter!

I Can't Believe I'm Not Bitter!

PAT FORTUNATO

"I Can't Believe I'm Not Bitter" by Pat Fortunato
ISBN-13: 978-0615673110

Published by Pat Fortunato and I Can't Believe I'm Not Bitter™
Publications, New York, NY

www.patnyc.com or **www.i-cant-believe-im-not-bitter.com**

pat4280@gmail.com
pat4280@aol.com

Printed by CreateSpace
Manufactured in the United States of America

For Lou, for all the obvious reasons.

I Can't Believe I'm Not Bitter!

Contents

Don't Listen to Anyone.
Except Me . . .

All that advice!

You've been getting it since birth and it will continue, unrelentingly, from here to eternity.

"Don't cry, things could be worse." All too true.

"A penny saved is a penny earned." Unless you factor in inflation.

"Live each day as if it were your last." And someday, you'll be right.

Wait, It Gets Worse!

We are now in the Golden Age of Self Esteem, so whenever you turn around, you are hit with advice like, *"You Can Do Anything!"* It makes me tired just to think about that.

And at the same time, The Brave New World of the Internet bombards you with cheery, inspirational messages like this one I just received:

"He who has health, has hope; and he who has hope, has everything."

Really? I thought that health wasn't that important. Silly me. Nice use of the semi-colon, though. You don't usually find such sophisticated punctuation in platitudes.

And all those books! "What to Expect When You're Not Expecting Anything," "How to Lose Lots of Weight Make Tons of Money and Find a Cure for Cancer in 10 Days or Less," "1001 Things Everyone Should Know about Life."

1001 things! You're kidding, right? I can't remember my own cell phone number half of the time. Maybe I could handle 500 ½ things. Probably not.

Add to all this free and not-so-free advice, we have the left-over gems from the Age of Aquarius like *This is the first day of the rest of your life,* and you're on inspirational overload.

I listen to all this well-meaning meddling—the platitudes, the proverbs, the old sayings, the new-age wisdom, the teachings of self-help gurus everywhere who yearn to make you a better human being—and all too often I find myself thinking,

"Yeah, but . . ."

Take the ubiquitous: *"You Can Do Anything!"*

I can?

Sure, I can accomplish a lot if I put my mind to it. I get that. I've done that. But *"Anything?"* Can I become a ballerina? Now? Not with these knees.

How about: "Live Your Life with No Regrets?" Can anyone actually do this? I mean, you're not allowed even one teensy weensy atom-sized regret? Einstein, for Pete's sake, didn't think his Greatest Hits were great enough.

But hold on a minute. Isn't some of this advice good?

Sure it is. Some of it. Some of the time. But as my doctor once told me (more advice!) about medical information on the web, only half of it is true—and how the hell do you know which half?

What's a body to do!

Relax, that's what. And when you hear yet another cliché that tells you how to live your life, remember these four little words:

"It Ain't Necessarily So."

Trust your own instincts a little more and listen to the "experts" a little less. It's okay to listen to me: I don't pretend to be an expert. I'm just a woman who doesn't always do things by the book. (Other books.) And has been known to bend, if not break, the rules. Yet somehow, I manage to muddle through. Without getting bitter!

So can you. Go forth and read the following short and not always sweet pieces. Each one questions a well-worn piece of advice, proving that you too can bend the rules without destroying the Great Cosmic Space-Time Continuum. Unless you want to. (See Yo, Universe, page 207.)

Now read the stories already. And see if you don't feel better.

You may even find yourself saying:

I Can't Believe I'm Not Bitter!

My Night at the Pussy Cat Lounge

66 Do something out of your comfort zone. **99**

I think whoever said this meant something like try seeded rye instead of whole wheat, or take the express train and walk 3 blocks instead of sitting longer on the local.

I, of course, took this advice too literally and went out —I mean, way out—of my comfort zone, not to mention my neighborhood. Once I got to the Pussy Cat Lounge, however, there was no turning back. . . .

My Night at the Pussy Cat Lounge

It wasn't a dark and stormy night.

Although things did get a tad turbulent in the course of the evening. It began, in fact, on a lovely spring day. . . .

A few months before our story begins, at a time in my life when I should have known better, I met a man on a plane on the way to California. I was developing a cold, a bad one, and he had a flask of whiskey (I should have been suspicious already), which he shared with me to help me get through the flight.

Although I told him that I was seeing someone seriously, we exchanged numbers and back in New York had a very pleasant lunch together. He was an ex-cop and was working as security chief at a major midtown hotel. He said that he understood that I was involved with someone else, but liked the company of good-looking women, and just wanted to do lunch.

A few weeks later, on that lovely spring day I told you about, I agreed to another lunch date. And since I was working hard in those days, I figured that I could make it late and take the rest of the day off. Well, by the time he called, it was really, really late, for lunch anyway, but I was hungry, overworked, and far too agreeable.

I agreed, therefore, to meet him at an address downtown I was unfamiliar with, left my office and grabbed a cab. The cabbie pulled up to the address I had been given, turned around and asked, just like in the movies, "Lady, are you sure this is the place?"

I wasn't sure at all: it was a dive called The Pussy Cat Lounge, a bona fide strip joint, with a long, low-lighted bar, and a stage on the left as you entered, featuring a woman doing what looked like the bridge position with benefits (not physical therapy as I know it), wearing a bad attitude—and very little else.

It's a not a good sign when the first thing you see in a public place is pubic space. And "crotch" is not the first word you think of for a restaurant review.

Do something out of your comfort zone—yes, well, this was pretty uncomfortable. So I strode to the bar, wearing a business suit and a confident air, which was a total joke, and asked for the guy I was supposed to meet, thinking all the while that this was a Big Fat Misunderstanding. It wasn't. Not only was he meeting me here, at this bar in this very unsavory place, he was part owner of the joint, and, as I later found out, not just an ex-cop, but an ex-cop who had been asked to leave the force. Uh-oh.

I bellied up to the bar (what else could a girl do) and pretended that this wasn't really weird. The bartender told me that he-who-shall-remain-nameless (we could call him He-Who for short) was running late and that I should have a drink on the house. I did. Several. And, lucky for me, they were watered down, because I was determined not to leave (I don't know why, but this had become a point of honor or something), and I kept drinking. There was no food. Not even a pretzel, unless you count some of the performers.

The women who were doing their thing across the way would come up to the bar between acts, so to speak, and when they found out I was in publishing would tell me their life stories. And interesting stories they were.

One of them was working her way through business school by performing a routine that involved not only whips and chains but also a very severe haircut and scary-looking handcuffs. Boy, was she going to be some strict boss! Another was getting away from an abusive spouse by wiggling her ass for drunken Wall Street types who were only too happy to show their support by shoving ten-dollar bills in the costume she almost had on. A would-be actress took this gig because the auditions for more, shall we say, traditional roles weren't exactly panning out, and all the directors wanted to do was, well you know.

We all drank Scotch together, enjoyed lots of girl talk, and I told them to send me outlines of the books they wanted to write. Thank Zeus, none of them ever did. I published children's books!

Finally, my "date" showed up, but by that time I was convinced he didn't just want lunch. (*Duh.*) Somehow, before I was too drunk to descend into total madness, I made a phone call. To the new man in my life. The one I was seeing seriously. And without missing a beat, he got the address and appeared on the scene, all Mr. Steady as He Goes, which, lord knows, I wasn't.

So how often do you get to be a damsel in distress? And then, how often do you get rescued?

Not that often.

I knew that night that my guy was a keeper. He sized up the situation, he didn't get upset, and Mr. Plane Person, AKA He-Who, knew he wasn't going anywhere anytime soon.

In the course of that strangely enchanted evening, we saw a woman perform an act that involved fire coming out of an orifice I'd rather not specify, and heard many more tales of woe. And we saw plenty of dough. The performers needed it, the customers paid it: a whole lot of money for a little Scotch, a lotta crotch. No one was complaining, just explaining. It was all very educational. Very educational.

He-Who asked me what it would take for me to get on stage and do my thing, and I said, A million two, cash. I have no idea where I came up with that figure, but co-owner or not, Mr. I-Just-Wanna-Have-Lunch wasn't coming up with that kind of money, so we'll never know if I would have done it or not.

But if I had done it, what would *it* have been? (It would have been hard to top the flaming orifice.) And how far out of my comfort zone would *that* have taken me? And would I be here to tell you this story? We'll never know—and I'm comfortable with that.

I've Lost It:
Law & Disorder

66 A place for everything,
and everything in its place. **99**

Oh, if only. I can't get by a single day—or hour—without misplacing something in my own apartment. I don't even know if these things are merely misplaced or truly lost. Whatever. It's a real nuisance.

I had pretty much resigned myself to the situation until I had an idea. A crazy idea, but hey, it just might work . . .

I've Lost It: Law & Disorder

"Detectives of *Law & Order*, listen up! I want to hire you, **ASAP**, to search my apartment. No, not for incriminating evidence, although that depends on how you define "incriminating," but to find all the things Missing In Inaction (MII) that I have abandoned hope of ever finding. You guys always find everything!"

Think about it, folks.

When these detectives search a place for evidence—a ticket to Tahiti or a gun, smoking or otherwise—they find the damn thing in mere moments. "What do we have here, Lenny? Looks like the professor is planning a little sabbatical."

Or, the exact opposite happens: they don't find what they're looking for—and are absolutely sure it isn't there. "The place is clean, Elliott. Let's take a look at the car."

I, on the other hand, can't find things for hours, days, years, decades, and in a few sad cases, forever. That poignant phrase, *"I know it's here someplace,"* can be heard echoing endlessly throughout the kingdom.

The MII items here at my place are not tickets to Tahiti (I should live so long) or guns (the only weapons I have are cooking knives, which are rarely sharpened). But whatever they are, the cops should have no trouble succeeding where I have failed. "Hey, Logan, have you seen my travel iron, last used in 1996?" Or the travel alarm clock, which probably went missing about the same time as the iron. Mr. Big, I assure you, can toss my crib any day.

How about the tape measure that is "always" in the hall closet, except when it isn't? Or the one remaining hot plate that isn't cracked? (I had dozens of these at one time.) The heating pad? The group photo from the Millennium party that was on the shelf for ten years, but has now mysteriously disappeared? It was in a frame and everything.

And the Misses Just Keep on Coming. . .

Where's the remote? My nail file? My keys? Yes, these items are small, but these guys find hairs and hairpins (DNA! DNA!). And while they're looking, what about the heart-shaped bookmark from Tiffany's? And the robin's-egg-blue-pen? The gold and green eye shadow I used this New Year's Eve? I really liked that.

Okay, someone may have taken the bookmark and the pen (unlikely, but possible), but who would walk off with that ratty heating pad? They're here someplace, dammit!

The detectives are also good with paperwork. A suspicious bill from Guns R Us or a receipt from the One Night Stand Motel doesn't stand a chance when they're on the case. Okay, guys. Go directly to the office. In the closet you'll find the File Cabinet from Hell and in it, somewhere, are things I'd pay real money to find, including the manual for the ancient TV in the den so I can figure out how to turn off the closed caption feature, and the list of restaurants in Paris for a friend who's going there this week. (I smell overtime pay on this one.)

Actually, I'd Like to Keep the Entire Staff(s) of *L&O* on Retainer.

We could call it The Lost & Found Unit—and I could contact them night and day for emergencies. Like losing the envelope I just had in my hands (IN MY HANDS!) five minutes ago (FIVE MINUTES AGO!) I've searched all over. Retraced my steps. To the kitchen. The bathroom. The closet where I was foraging around for gum, which I also didn't find. The stack of newspapers. My purse, where it had been earlier.

I can't find an envelope I had five minutes ago—but they find evidence from years ago, which may or may not exist and if it does, could be anywhere in the universe. I realize there's a difference between Life and TV, but this is ridiculous. I just know that Vincent D'Onofrio could tilt his head the way he does (that man must require serious chiropractic care) and tell me where—and why!—I lost the letter. He knows everything.

Maybe I should see a shrink: Am I losing all these things instead of my mind? Because I harbor hidden hostility to heating pads and hot plates? To create confusion so that I don't have to think about real problems, such as why I watch all those episodes of *Law & Order* in the first place? Is there a void in my life that I am trying to fill with reruns? Hell. Where is Doctor Wong when you need him!

Or maybe this is a purely practical problem of too much stuff/not enough space because I insist on living in Manhattan. Since most versions of *Law & Order* take place in the city, the cops are usually searching apartments, not houses. And that's directly linked to my problem. Although on the surface the opposite might seem true, it's actually much easier to lose things in smaller living spaces.

You have no attic, basement, or garage to store things in, so you have to pack everything, densely, in boxes and drawers, under the bed, under the sofa, behind the sofa, jammed in closets and cabinets, high and low, all on one floor, yes, but in a few rooms so crammed with things that you can't bring in a deck of cards without destroying the delicate ecological balance.

And yet. I do suspect that there actually is some underlying psychological cause for all this losing of things and searching for things.

It must have something to do with sex. What am I searching for that's lost? My youth? My virginity? Okay, that's a stretch, but I just know that Olivia would understand.

I finally found the envelope. It was buried in the bedclothes. See? I told you it had sexual undertones.

Hmm. What if . . . I became a suspect in a crime. Would they let me watch while the cops searched my apartment? Would they find the hairbrush? The iridescent eye shadow? Would they get cranky if I mentioned the travel iron?

Look on the bright side; if all these things actually are in my apartment, then they're not truly lost, only misplaced. What if I devoted a day, or two, or however long it took, to sifting through all my stuff? Would I find anything interesting? Incriminating? Things I forgot I had? Would I get all nostalgic and start Googling people I've lost track of? You lose people, too, although seldom without a trace. Maybe Anthony LaPaglia could help. Love his face.

Maybe, just maybe, I would actually throw away some junk like I did when the kitchen was remodeled. I hardly ever lose anything in there anymore except the knife sharpener and the hot plate. Could this level of organization coexist peacefully in the entire apartment? Would I find the tape measure? The heart-shaped bookmark?

And what would I do with all the time I now spend looking for things? Would I write more? Would people laugh? Is that a good thing?

Frankly, detectives, I don't have a clue.

My Free Gift
from Estee Lauder

66 Do something nice for yourself. **99**

Well, why not? You deserve it, right? You're tense and stressed from all the work you do, for others, of course. And what could be wrong with giving yourself a little present now and then?

I'll tell you what. You could spend a lot of time and a fair amount of money and end up more tense and stressed than you were before. Here's my sad story:

My Free Gift
from Estee Lauder

What do women want? Love? Sure. Money? Of course. Cosmetics? Now you're talking! Comedienne Rita Rudner nails it in her very funny routine about those "free gifts"— you know the ones, where you buy something you don't need to get a bunch of things you don't want.

I can rationalize falling for this a few summers ago because I was recovering from surgery, and hey, a girl needs a "free gift" at a time like that. Of course, I can rationalize anything, but honestly, that ad was so enticing. The cutest little pink-and-white checkered cosmetic case filled with goodies like summer blush (I need that: It's summer! I'm pale!) plus various and sundry creams and lotions with intriguing names.

My Italian grandmother believed that all the dishwashing liquids, shampoos, and just about any product in a bottle, were all exactly the same thing in different colors with different names. I do wonder about New Dawn versus Herbal Essence (They're even the same shade of green), and I am totally baffled by all those skin creams.

Do I really need a different moisturizer for under my eyes, my throat, my t-zone, the rest of my face? For summer, winter, spring or fall, night or day? Light, extra light, rich, super rich, fabulously firming, with aloe, lanolin, collagen, gentian, pearl drops of moisture, invigorating enzymes, hydrating hormones and unspecified ingredients that revitalize, rejuvenate, relax, and restore?

And yet.

I Love Those Little Kits with the Goodies.

And so, without further ado (that would come later), I cut out the ad from Macy's in *The New York Times* and called the toll-free number. But after three or four attempts to place my order, involving several of those delightful telephone trees, I was told that no one there knew anything about the ad, and was advised to call the Macy's in New York. I should have scrapped the project at that point, but I had a little time on my hands, and recuperating can be kind of grim, and damn it, I wanted that little pink cosmetic case.

So I called Macy's. And called Macy's. And left messages. And dealt with trees. And spoke to half a dozen women, some with names I couldn't pronounce, and one whose name, left on my answering machine, was impossible to decipher. She was calling to tell me that my credit card wasn't going through. I knew the card was okay, but I called Master Card, then Macy's again, and left messages, and was finally told by What's-Her-Name that I should really come into the store to get the gift.

I wasn't fully recovered. I couldn't leave the house. This purchase was supposed to cheer me up. It was making me feel worse. I gave her my American Express card number and hoped for the best.

Three weeks later, when the goodies still hadn't arrived (She Who Cannot Be Pronounced had said it would take 5 to 7 business days), I finally gave up on the whole thing and threw the ad away. I was feeling better; I could get the lipstick somewhere else.

And then I got the bill from American Express and saw the $40.21 charge for the stuff I had never received. The noive! I called Macy's. Again. I was referred to many more fascinating people, including Carol, Susan, Edilma and Muffy, who was the manager, James Gray, the Chief Operating Officer, and someone even higher up on the cosmetics chain named Corinne, the last in a long line of personnel who only wanted to help and serve me.

I begged Corinne to just cancel the charge. The hell with the promise of new youth and beauty, just give me my money back. But she insisted that, for my convenience, the best course of action would be to have the gift delivered. She even promised to send it the next day, a Thursday. Which came and went, with no sign of the package. When I called Corinne, my new BFF, she promised I'd get it first thing Monday, and so on Tuesday I called again.

Corinne was upset. She said that she tried to deliver the package herself (Hey! What are friends for?) but couldn't find my building. A simple enough mistake considering that it takes up nearly a city block and anybody could walk right past it. RIIIIGHT. She promised to deliver it the next day, and, three days later, on Friday, it did finally arrive.

Of course, it was the wrong free gift. There was no blush, and the free lipsticks were the wrong color. And there were some dumb eye shadows no one could possibly need or want.

Sigh. No cute little pink-and-white bag, which Corinne had told me was not pink anyway but was actually red, but I hadn't believed her and was secretly hoping for pink. Instead there was one big beachy kind of blue bag (not bad, but not pink) containing two smaller bags (kind of mauve) with all the stuff I could definitely live without.

Well, I kept everything (I wasn't going to send it back!), and hopefully I am wiser for the experience.

Here's What I Learned:

• "Free gift" is redundant, and therefore, suspicious. If it's free, it has to be a gift. If it's a gift, it has to be free. It can't be a free purchase, or a gift that you pay for. Supreme Court Judge Antonin Scalia made the same point in On Language in *The Sunday Times*. Imagine! Scalia and me (or is it I?) together at last, and I read it in *The Times*.

• Nevertheless, that something is advertised in a full-page ad in *The New York Times* means absolutely nothing.

• Immediately abandon a project when you have to deal with more than one telephone tree at more than one number, and/or are referred to a manager named Muffy.

• Thinking Pink doesn't always work.

• In short, although I have always identified with *The Little Engine That Could*, sometimes You Just Can't. I have a feeling that this new attitude will serve me well when dealing with contractors, plumbers, cable repair people, reservation clerks, the Long Island Expressway, and certain sections of Southern New Jersey.

• And the saddest lesson of all:
Trying to do something nice for yourself isn't as easy as it sounds.

But a girl can't let these things get her down. It's a sunny day, and I am taking my big blue bag and going to the beach. And if my lipstick melts, so what? I hear they're having this great offer for a free gift at Bloomingdale's . . .

The Eleven Stages
of Packing

66 Travel light. **99**

How many times have you heard this? And how many times, struggling madly to get on a crowded train, plane, or in a (midget-sized) automobile with two gigantic suitcases and The Purse That Ate Cleveland have you wished you had followed this perfectly reasonable advice?

Why didn't you? Because it's just too hard, that's why.

The Eleven Stages of Packing

Yes, yes, I know. Grief has only seven stages, but this is more complicated.

Stage 1: *Regret: Why am I taking this trip?*

Why? Because it's a cruise on the Queen Mary 2 (a dream of mine), that's why, and it leaves from Brooklyn, a cab ride away. No plane! No security lines! No being trapped in a flying sardine can with people who mess up the bathroom in unspeakable ways!

It does seem pretty petty to complain about having to pack. But for me, packing is always traumatic.

Stage 2: *Oh come on, it can't be that hard.*

In an episode of *Mad Men*, Betty accompanied Dan to Rome at the last minute, and arrived looking as if she had stepped out of a "beauty parlor," with a stunning outfit for every occasion. Characters in fiction tend to have little luggage and unlimited wardrobes and spend mere minutes throwing things in a suitcase and getting on with it.

True, on *Sex and The City*, Carrie does agonize about packing for Paris (How does a girl choose between all those Manolo Blahniks?) and ends up with a lot of luggage. But the sheer number of ultra-chic, complicated outfits she wears couldn't have fit in all the luggage at Suitcases R Us, or on the plane itself—even if the other passengers voluntarily offered to give her their spaces. The gorgeous pale grey formal gown alone would have required a steamer trunk.

Stage 3: Panic.

I realize that this is The Real World, not TV or the movies, and it IS that hard . . .

Stage 4: The making of the lists.

This calms me down momentarily because I have the illusion of being in control, and at this point I realize I already have most of what I need. But "most" is not "all," so it sends me back to Stage 3, thinking of having to go shopping for the rest of the stuff.

Stage 5: The shopping.

The first piece of clothing I get, cream crepe pants so that I won't be in black every single evening, turns out to be the last thing, because department stores are just too confusing and trigger yet more panic. Then there are cosmetics and all the drugstore items, which have lists of their own and will be purchased at the last minute. See Stages 3 and 4.

Stage 6: Asking for advice.

People give you well-meaning but somewhat contradictory advice like: Don't bring too much—but yes, you must take that smashing red dress even though you will wear it once. Solution: Don't ask for advice.

Stage 7: Taken to the cleaners.

I realize that whatever I bring had better be clean, so I sort out stuff to wash or send to the cleaners, and this gives me a false sense of security, of Having Gotten Something Done. But this quickly dissolves into . . .

Stage 8: Whoops! I forgot about that!

This is when I realize that I've forgotten about something significant, like the swimming pool onboard, which requires bringing bathing suits (oh nooo), a coverup, and flip-flops. It's winter. Where did I put those things?

Stage 9: My life is a mess.

Packing forces me to face the fact that my closets are a disaster, and that to find something in the apartment will take all the detectives of *Law & Order* and then some. (See *I've Lost It* on page 13.) It also forces me to admit that I can't wear 90% of the cute shoes in those disorganized closets because I can't walk in them. On land, much less on sea.

Stage 10: The moment of truth.

I have to pack because I'm leaving tomorrow, and nobody else is going to do it for me.

Now I am a whirling dervish, grabbing clothes out of the closet and shoes from their boxes, laying out everything on the bed, picking and choosing, putting the things that didn't make the cut into shopping bags to be dealt with "later," and somehow, packing it all in, literally.

The case is closed, so to speak. Between now and the minute it goes out the door, there will be doubts, additions, subtractions, and substitutions. But once I'm in the taxi, it's like sitting down to take a test. You've done everything you can, now let it rip.

Stage 11: *Acceptance*: *I did the best I could.*

Leaving my building I already know, or think I know, some of the mistakes I've made. Why didn't I bring those new sandals (which, it will turn out, I didn't need), and why did I take that extra shawl (which, it will turn out, I ended up wearing every night).

But it's too late. It's a *fait accompli*. I probably have too much of some things, made a few reckless choices, but will have pretty much what I need. And what I've forgotten, I'll either do without or buy on the ship.

Besides, you may be familiar with that other great platitude: A hopeful heart and an open mind are the best traveling companions . . . Yeah, but I also need my stuff.

Bring Colace

66 Be Prepared. 99

Okay, so you just found out that traveling light is an oxymoron. Besides, when you take a trip, you also must remember the good old Boy Scout's motto and bring the things that are absolutely necessary.

The problem is, how do you know what that will be? How do you prepare for every eventuality? On my next trip, I tried to remember everything, and managed to forget the one thing I really, really needed to keep my vacation from going down the toilet . . .

Bring Colace

Oh, the indignities of travel . . .

The e-mail message from Rome was brief and to the point:
Bring Colace.

The instant reply from New York was equally succinct:
Relief is on the way!

What's the story behind these messages between the Old Country and the New World? Isn't Italy famous for great gelato and naked statues? Pizza and piazzas? Pizza in the piazza? What does Colace have to do it?

Aspetta, my friend, *aspetta*.

First of all, when the travelers in question are not twenty, Colace is not the lone indignity. It begins with the irony of the luggage. You can lift less, but you need more. Your little kit with aspirin and toothpaste has slowly evolved into a bewildering assortment of items, including . . .

Your reading glasses and your other glasses for TV, so that with your sunglasses you have three pairs to lose; your contact lenses, their case(s) and solution(s); your prescription medicines plus the painkiller of your choice, maybe that new stuff that you rub directly into your forehead.

Of course you need shampoo and conditioner (your hair is dry), gel or spray (it's unruly, too), and something for sleep.

But wait! Don't forget the tweezers for geezers, an absolute necessity since you've taken to sprouting hairs in places other than your eyebrows.

If You're a Woman

You can add a shitload, you should pardon the expression, of creams and cosmetics because even a "natural" look requires foundation, blush, eye shadow, mascara, eyeliner, eyebrow pencil, lip liner, and—you can't survive jet lag without it— concealer. You don't use each of these every day, and you may go without makeup a lot of the time, but you will need some of these things at some point, so how the hell do you know which not to take?

And Then There Are the Shoes . . .

I knew a lot about Italy before this trip, and love the Italians, many of whom seem to be my relatives. They are nice people. They encourage me to speak their language, which must be painful to their fine Italian ears, and I love their *lasagna alla Bolognese*.

But Italians have no concept of convenience and this, too, can lead to indignities. Take the cobblestones. Please. For Americans, they are impossible to walk on in anything resembling nice-looking shoes. So you wear clodhoppers. Then you notice that the only other human in Italy with shoes as ugly as yours is the nun in a cathedral, the one with a mustache (She's home. She has tweezers. What's her problem?) and the hideous haircut that only a Mother Superior could love. There was one other example of really bad shoes. But when I looked up with a glimmer of hope, it turned out to be a man, bearded and begging for Euros in the streets of Bologna.

Before you tell me that I am full of the same, trust me on this: all Italian women, unless they are ANCIENT, wear good-looking shoes. They are genetically engineered with both the desire to possess good leather and the ability to walk in fabulous shoes in impossible conditions.

I wanted to announce to the world that I have cute shoes, too. But the truth is that I'm not young enough to wear them for actual walking. I might as well admit that, because you can't travel without revealing your age. Yet another indignity! First it's your passport for the nosy clerks in the hotels. Then it's your international driver's license, which you forget in the glove compartment of your Italian cousin's car. Oh well, now the relatives know why I can't wear cute shoes.

But about the Colace. . .

Thinking about the beauty of Italy is almost enough to make me forget about that nasty episode of the, you should pardon the expression, stool softener, which I may add is an absolute must in Italy where the diet has lots of *pasta, prosciutto,* and *formaggio,* and precious little fiber. So I better get this over with.

Suffice it to say that during my trip I got to know various and sundry bathrooms intimately, giving new meaning to the phrase Fleet Week. Talk about indignity! Some people do these things for pleasure? Are they out of their minds? Anyway, when everything settled down and I just needed a little help, I was forced to do one of two things:

1) Attempt to explain to a pharmacist, in Italian, what the hell Colace is. It's not exactly a laxative, you see. And I know from experience that if you ask for a *lasativo* you will get a high-octane product that will knock the you-know-what out of you, which makes sense given the local diet.

2) Send an e-mail to a friend who was meeting us and ask her for help. Indignity was not an issue here: we've been through worse things in the past. Don't ask.

The decision to go for number two, so to speak, produced the infamous "Bring Colace" e-mail, so the solution to my problem turned out to be just a click away.

I have to go now—and, hopefully, tomorrow, and tomorrow, and the next day, but I think we have all learned some valuable lessons today that we can take with us in our travels.

Bring Colace—it gives a whole new meaning to traveling light.

Oh! You're Supposed to Throw *Coins*!!

66 Always wear clean underwear. 99

Listen to yo mama on this one, my friends. You never know what the day will bring.

Although if your intimate apparel is too clean—or too nice—you could get into trouble. I know. It happened to me. But before you judge me too harshly, listen to my story.

Oh! You're Supposed to Throw *Coins*!!

I am capable of losing anything. Gloves, of course, and also pens, pencils, cell phones, keys, wallets and address books. You know, the usual. But am I satisfied parting with those everyday items that any fool could lose? Not I. Perhaps I was cursed at birth by a vindictive gypsy (perhaps I've been watching too many operas) who foretold that I would be able to misplace any thing, any place, any time.

I could tell you about the senior thesis on obscure Irish poets that I lost and had to rewrite, but I'm sure you'd much rather hear about the time I lost my underwear in the vicinity of the Trevi Fountain in Rome.

How Can You Lose Your Underwear, You May Ask?

You may ask. And I shall answer.

I was in Italy with my friend and we went shopping for tennis outfits at this really nice store near the Trevi Fountain. They had good prices (that was back in the day when a dollar wasn't worth 66 cents), with quality brands, and we had a ball trying on everything the cute Italian clerk kept handing us through the curtains of the teeny little fitting room. He did seem to be lingering a little too long, and leaning a little too far in, but, hey, this was Italy. Each of us bought a few outfits, some of which I still use today, and so, mission accomplished, we hurried off in search of gelato.

Later that day around cocktail hour, my friend, her husband and I were gathered together at the piano bar of the very chic Hotel Hassler. I know, I know, that's a German name, but trust me, it's a very fancy Italian hotel at the top of the Spanish Steps.

So anyway, there we were, the three of us, working our Campari and sodas on my last evening in Rome—they were staying a few more days. As the piano quietly tinkled in the background, and elegant Italians (elegant Italians are really, really elegant) talked politely over cocktails and delicious little nibbly things, I asked my friends if they thought they'd be going back to the Trevi. If so, I wondered, could they stop in that sweet little store and see if anyone had found my underwear?

After the explosion of "Wots!" that issued forth simultaneously from the two of them, there seemed, at least to me, to be total silence in the room. Even the piano player stopped in the middle of "People."

Well, maybe it was the drinks, or that When in Rome Feeling, or maybe it was just me, accustomed practically from birth to losing all manner of things, but I didn't think it was that big a deal.

In the shop, I had been wearing my favorite cream-colored camisole and tap pants set—silk, lace, the whole nine yards:

actually, very little in the way of yardage, but very effective in the lacy lingerie department. God knows who I thought I would meet later in that great city that fine day. Or night. Or maybe I just felt like wearing pretty lingerie. It was Rome. I was free and over . . . twenty-one.

Anyway, I was wearing a bra and pantyhose underneath the sensuous silk set, so when I got dressed (remember, it was very cramped quarters—and I was tired from all that shopping!), I guess I forgot to put on the cami and pants. Whoops.

The next day, I took off for New York, and my friends took off for the Little Shop of Panties, down by the Trevi, where the very good-looking young man who had been helping us (and perhaps himself) claimed that *no, no signori,* of course he had not found anything like the intimate articles being described to him by this crazy American couple.

My friends left the shop empty handed, and went to the fountain to throw in a few coins. You're supposed to do that, you probably know, to insure that you'll return to Rome.

But you have to wonder. If throwing coins in the Trevi brings you back to Rome, what happens if you leave your underwear in that vicinity?

Do your panties become expantriots? Will you be extradited from the U.S. and hauled back to the Eternal City on charges of lewd and indecent behavior? Or will you return and have a hot affair with the cute clerk? He's the perfect age by now.

Whatever. But that young man knew more than what he

was telling. Much more. It is my firm belief (it's so nice to have something firm these days) that somewhere in Rome, perhaps on this very day, some woman is riding around on a Vespa wearing my cami and tap pants.

I just hope they're clean.

Who Was That Countess at Harry's Bar?

66 Be yourself. **99**

A cocktail napkin I use adds this: "Everyone else is taken."
Wise words to live by—most of the time. But is it ever all right to pretend to be someone you're not? Personally, I think it's imperative. In certain situations. And who do you believe, a cocktail napkin or me. . . .

Who Was That Countess at Harry's Bar?

It was I. Well, sort of.

My husband and I were staying in Venice in a swanky hotel, with a staff more than willing to satisfy our every whim.

Actually, I was pretty whimless, except for one thing: I wanted to go to the famous Harry's Bar—and I wanted a good table. I had heard that if you were banished to the back room, you might as well skip the whole thing.

In my mangled Italian, I conveyed to the exceedingly cute desk clerk (in Italy, aren't they all?) what I wanted. He nodded knowingly, made the reservation, and gave us a card with a note to the effect that Mr. & Mrs. Us were honored guests of the Bauer Hotel. This was code for: Give them a good table.

And so, that night, dressed in our one "good" traveling outfit: basic black with (real) pearls for me, blue blazer, grey pants and a tie from Ferragamo for him, we strolled to Harry's Bar. Note: In Italy, you stroll, not walk.

Prego . . .

Harry's Bar looked quiet on the outside, but inside, it was a zoo. The bar was loaded with assorted Eurotrash, including one young couple who couldn't keep their hands off each other.

While I was trying to figure out how to negotiate this scene, my husband, who isn't intimidated by these sorts of things, calmly handed the card from the hotel to the guy who looked like he was in charge, saying simply, *"Prego."*

That did the trick.

We were shown to a tiny table across from the bar, probably the best in the house. But I, still a bit dazed and going into princess mode, noted that it was a very small table—which, rather than annoying the maitre d' or whoever he was, made him take us more seriously. Who the hell was this picky person, he had to wonder.

Is That Gore Vidal Over There?

After being cajoled into accepting the great but small table and ordering the required Bellinis, I looked around and saw that all the tables were tiny, except for one in the corner with a group of sophisticated-looking folks, including a man who looked a lot like the famous writer and curmudgeon, Gore Vidal.

Could it be Vidal? He lived in this general area of Italy, he must eat dinner, and he, too, had a good table. . . .

No, It's Ken Auletta!

Looking more closely, this guy was much younger than Gore and seemed, well, nicer. After a while, I figured out who he was: Ken Auletta, writer for *The New Yorker* and author of many bestselling books—most recently *Googled: The End of the World As We Know It.*

Meanwhile, I got distracted by the couple at the bar—he now had his hand down her jeans—and by the very elegant gentleman who sat down on our left. Obviously a regular, probably actual royalty with one of those palazzos on the canal, who, without looking at the menu, simply said in Italian, *"I'll have something light."* How cool is that. But on the other hand, with my grasp of the language, he may have said, *"Who the hell are these people sitting next to me?"*

We, too, ordered light, although from the menu. A little salad and some risotto. We split an entrée, even though the portions were small, and shared dessert. The bill came to $400. Which is, even now, the most expensive meal I've ever had — *per bite*.

It was worth every penny.

The Kid Gets in the Picture

We happened to be leaving at the same time as the Auletta party, and when we got outside, they were posing for a picture. Being the helpful little thing that I am, I asked Mr. A if he would like my husband to take the photo, but Ken, as I now like to call him, said no, they came with their own paparazzi (he was kidding), and that we should get in the picture (he wasn't kidding).

Then we all walked, or strolled, to St Mark's Piazza, which has to be the most beautiful outdoor living room on the planet, and on the way, the woman who turned out to be Ken's agent asked me if I was the Countess De Something Or Other.

I didn't really hear the name, having been shocked speechless by the question—literally, because I knew that once I opened my mouth, she'd know I was no Italian countess.

Miraculously, I managed to pull out something from deep within my would-be royal gut, and without pausing, said, simply, "If you wish."

I Should Have Said . . . What I Said.

"If you wish:" so tantalizing, so vague, so not exactly a lie. For me, that answer wiped out all the "I should have saids" on countless, if not countess, occasions. On several continents.

We all said goodbye at the piazza, air kisses and everything, and my husband and I returned to the Bauer, having gone to the famous Harry's Bar, having been made royalty by Ken Auletta's agent, and having been in a photo with him that must still exist somewhere in the universe. I only wish I knew the name of the royal personage I was mistaken for so I could look her up and see who I almost was.

But what the hell, you can't have everything. Even when you're a countess.

.

My Life on Post-its: Or, Who Are Larry & Chuck?

66 Write it down! 99

If you write everything down, it's supposed to help you to get organized. I'd like that. Of course, I'd also like to be Queen of Albania. But both aspirations seem equally out of my reach.

Nevertheless, I try. I take the advice of all those experts and write notes to myself all the time. Often on Post-its, which are so nice to slap on all sorts of things and come in all those cute colors and useful sizes. But are they really helping? Can anything? And in the grand scheme of things, does it matter . . . ?

My Life on Post-its: Or, Who Are Larry & Chuck?

I have absolutely no idea, although I've been wracking my brains for hours. Larry and Chuck Who? And what in the world does the notation "2nd" under their names signify?

I'd better figure it out soon because it's on my calendar for today.

It could mean almost anything, and that I can't think of a single Larry or a Chuck in my life is totally irrelevant. Second could be second floor. Where? In this building? At my gym? Somewhere in the city? Maybe I made an appointment to look at a wholesale leather jacket in the garment district, and Larry and Chuck are my guys. Maybe not. I haven't had a contact there in years, and the mediocre quality of my current jacket proves it.

Could it be a TV show? Yeah, but not even I would write 2nd, rather than Channel 2. Or chan2, which I could interpret as "change to." Change to—what? One thing it *can't* be is the 2nd of the month, because it was written in for the 9th. Maybe I missed the whole thing? Whatever the whole thing was.

Post-its, Pads, and Beyond

I leave notes to myself in every conceivable place, and not just on Post-its. (How did we manage before these sticky little wonders, I wonder.) I write on every manner of matter: my appointment book, sure, but also on pads, random pieces of paper, and in countless notebooks.

I am the crazy lady in the CVS pharmacy buying notebooks in every size, color, pattern, and type, all ostensibly for specific purposes, which invariably become hopelessly confused, so that notations for my daily notebook often end up in the financial notebook, which is green (for cash) and labeled $$$$$ just in case I forget, or in the Blog & I, Part Deux Notebook, not to be confused with the original Blog & I Notebook, a large pink spiral bound book with side pockets and a very jazzy cover. I even have notebooks, smaller though, and with plain covers, for various surgeries, including Gall-stones I Have Known and Into the Bowels of Hell.

In the kitchen I write on paper towels. In the bathroom on toilet paper: I usually find these, weeks later in the pocket of my bathrobe when it's about to be laundered. If I'm lucky. Many a note has been washed and dried, never to be deciphered again by human brains. Not even the guys on CSI could find meaning in these soapy scribblings after 2X Ultra Condensed Tide with Bleach gets through with them. Imagine if I used the 3X brand.

Cryptic, But Clear?

Some of these notes, the ones that escape the laundry room, actually are cryptic but clear—an oxymoron if ever I heard one. I mean, they're clear to me if not to the universe.

HC/C stands for hair cut and color. PT is for physical therapy. BC means Book Club.

MO means an opera at the Metropolitan Opera. Although MO could also mean Motive & Opportunity or Modus Operandi, either of which could lead to ponderings of life's myriad mysteries. I once had MO in my book and got all dressed up for the opera only to discover my new microwave oven was being delivered. (Impressed the hell out of the delivery guy.) But opera notes usually work for me, especially since I've gotten into the habit of putting little musical notes next to the letters. Even "M Butt," though terribly crude sounding for such moving music, was, clearly, *Madama Butterfly*.

How about the Post-it I found stuck to my computer a while back that said Pro War? Which I am emphatically not. It turned out to mean: Protest War, and now that I've deciphered it, I can explain.

I had decided that since kids on campuses aren't protesting all these lousy wars, then we geezers have to. I even have a name for us: Geezniks. So, when a rally was scheduled at the UN, I had made myself a note about it. I didn't go, I forget why—probably because I didn't write it down—but at least I knew where I was supposed to be.

As opposed to, say, Larry and Chuck's place, on 2nd. Ooh. Could that be 2nd Avenue? Yeah, it could. So what.

Grocery Post-its are really bad when you're standing in Aisle 3 staring blankly at that piece of paper in your hand. Something that looked like SOAPY LIQUOR turned out to be Ivory Liquid. Lucky thing my husband usually does the shopping.

Every day, I throw out unintelligible Post-its, scraps of paper, and the pages of those little notebooks where I have scribbled thoughts for articles, plans for travel, investment ideas, the names of people I'm supposed to get in touch with for something if only I could remember what. Now that I write a blog, I find notes like, "I came, I saw, I plotzed" on a square of toilet tissue. What kind of post did I have in mind when I wrote that? With any luck, we'll never know.

"Mermaid Con Isle"

Those were the words I found written in my appointment book one warm Saturday in May. This led to many pleasant thoughts. Was there a Mermaid Isle on the itinerary for today, I wondered, a place where mermaids tried to lure (con) you into doing . . . what? Something fun, for sure. Or was Mermaid Con Isle some new clothing line, involving cotton lisle (I could have so easily left off the L), a silky natural material? And natural is so in this season.

But maybe it was a new restaurant (even after that dreadful bout of food poisoning from eating those shrimp from the supermarket, I still love seafood.) And isn't there a Mermaid Inn in Manhattan? Was I supposed to meet someone named Connie there? Conrad, maybe? Or could "con" be Spanish for "with" and I was going there with . . . Isle? Or Lisle?

It could be the name of a rock group. Or a race horse. No weirder than Mine My Bird, and he won the derby in 2009! My horse had a much nicer name, Hold Me Back. Took it too seriously, though. He came in 12th.

I finally figured it out. It was the Mermaid Parade at Coney Island. Of course! What else could it have been! Might have been fun, too, but by now I was in the mood for a sea-food dinner. Preferably with a Spaniard wearing a silky shirt made from cotton lisle.

Girls Just Want to Have Fun
or At Least Eat Lobster Salad

But wait! I know who Larry and Chuck are!

Actually, it should have been Chuck and Larry, as in the movie, *I Now Pronounce You Chuck and Larry*. My brother, who was working on the film, had said they'd be shooting this morning on the 2nd floor of somewhere (never found out the location), and if I wanted to visit the set, I should call. By the time I had deciphered the note, though, it was too late.

Okay, so I've heard that the movie isn't all that great, but I like some of the music in it, and it would have been fun to meet Larry and Chuck, AKA Chuck and Larry, AKA Kevin James and Adam Sandler. Maybe we would have hit it off, and could have drifted off together to the Mermaid Parade—or, better yet, the Mermaid Inn for a couple of beers.

Of course, I'd have to find the address of the place first, which I always forget. Quick! Hand me a Post-it! Got to make a note of that.

The
DO-NOT-DO List

66 Make a list. 99

This is an offshoot of "write it down." And we know how well that worked out.

    Lists, they say, bring order to chaos, relieve stress, and focus the mind. According to a well-known sociologist who should know, they "get to the heart of what it is we need to do to get through another day on this planet."

    Oh yeah? What if you can't get to all the things on your To Do list? What if most of your list for Monday becomes your list for Tuesday, and the whole thing makes you wonder how you're going to get through Wednesday? On this planet. I have another way to relieve stress and focus the mind. It's a list, all right. But it's called:

The DO-NOT-DO List

Tear up your TO DO list right now and replace it with a DO-NOT-DO list.

No, really. It's important for your mental health.

In *Get Him to the Greek,* Russell Brand says the great thing about doing drugs is that you always have only one thing on your TO DO list: *Get drugs.*

Although I'd never suggest anything more addictive than a few martinis for medicinal purposes, having only one thing on your TO DO list sure beats the wretchedly long lists the rest of us face each and every day.

The only good thing about TO DO lists is the perverse pleasure of checking off an item you've completed. I like that part. In an obsessive-compulsive sort of a way. But it's cold comfort, really, because you never, ever get to check everything off. And that leads to the depressing question: What the hell did I do today?

My friend Sarah says that nobody ever completes more than 80% of their list, no matter how simple or difficult the items are. She's right. I have put "Wash hair" or " Check the weather" on the list some days, just to give myself something to cross off, but it doesn't help. I get 80% done, if I'm lucky.

And yet. We all make lists.

So, If You Don't Want to Turn to Narcotics, and You Don't, There's Only One Solution: The DO-NOT-DO list.

It's easy to make . . .

Think of things you're *not* going to do today, or possibly ever, and write them down.

The list can include broad issues like:

• I will not discover the meaning of life (we can safely assume that won't happen any time soon).

Or specific actions like:

• I won't go to the Post Office and I will not Go Postal: This is a good one, because you have two choices: You can either not go to the Post Office, or you can go there and not Go Postal. If that's possible.

Best of all are outright impossibilities, such as:

• I will not grow my hair 3 inches today. Cross that one off immediately.

My own personal list includes such goodies as . . .

• I will not re-organize The Drawer from Hell in the kitchen. (A little clutter never hurt anyone.)

• I will not believe the guy at the all-night deli who says that the flowers are fresh when they look wilted.

(Long sentences like this are satisfying to cross out.)

• I will not try to understand the book I am alleged-
ly reading called *The Twenty-Seventh City*. (Maybe a
second reading will bring comprehension, but that's
something I will not do today.)

Now, it's your turn to make up your very own Do-Not-Do
List.

Go on, it's fun. And here are a few suggestions:

• You won't call your sister-in-law.

• You won't clean out the hall closet.

• You won't go to the gym, the dentist, make your will,
or file your taxes.

Then, at the end of the day, you get to check off all the
things you haven't done. And make another DO-NOT-DO list
for tomorrow.

On the other hand, if you absolutely can't break yourself
of the habit of making those odious TO-DO lists that you've
been doing all these years, and they are addictive, there's one
other solution.

Make the damn list, but with only one word on it: "Nothing." And nothing . . . could be easier. And you'll get 100% of
it done. I promise.

Sounds Like a Plan: The Art of Procrastination

66 Never put off 'till tomorrow what you can do today. 99

Right. Except for one thing—ever notice that some things you put off kind of disappear on their own after a while? The exhibit closes. The sale is over. The last bill has been added to your current bill. And what if, god forbid, you get hit by a bus tomorrow, why do your taxes today?

If you're putting something off, it means that you really don't want to do it, and to quote another platitude I find so much more useful: "Life is short." So why spend your limited time on this planet doing something you don't want to do—when you may never have to do it at all?

Sounds Like a Plan:
The Art of Procrastination

You gotta have a plan, or you'll never be able to procrastinate in peace.

Say you don't want to go to that exhibit at the Met, the one everyone says you absolutely positively must see. Your cultural creds depend on it!

Here's what you must do: write it down in your date book with as much sincerity as you can muster. When you get to that date—make it far enough in advance as possible so that many things can crop up—you will almost certainly be busy with other, more urgent things. But you can say with a straight face that you were planning to go and had to miss it, thus fulfilling your obligation to Art and The Finer Things of Life. And avoiding the dreaded admission, "I should have gone, but I didn't."

As Stuart Smiley would say, you "should" all over yourself all the time. This has got to stop. If you don't have a plan, these "shoulds" can nag you incessantly, and your unconscious guilt will bubble up to the surface and drown you.

Take a Hike!

What if you find yourself blurting out something like, Why don't we see that show—or make those brownies or take that hike—this weekend? That's okay if you say it early enough in the week, preferably Monday. Something is bound to come up that messes up plans for the weekend. Saying anything after Wednesday is dicey. However, if pushed, promising to go the following weekend usually works. Indefinitely.

Are you getting the idea? As long as you have a plan, you can procrastinate forever.

But shows, brownies, and even hikes are easy things to procrastinate about, just examples to get us started on this little known but crucial concept. Now let's look at something harder, like a trip to the Antarctic.

A What to Where?

According to the fancy travel magazine I get from American Express, all the cool people are going to Antarctica this year. I actually met a woman at a party who specializes in tours there. Now, I like to travel as much as anyone, but Antarctica? Forget cool. It's *cold* down there. Really cold. What happened to the year when everyone was going to Spain? Barcelona is sooo nice. You could plan a trip there and actually go. In fact, you should.

Meanwhile, there are those pesky thoughts of Antarctica, which could, if left unchecked, cost you your peace of mind.

Let's face it, some part of you does want to fly down to Penguinville. You might not be the very first kid on your block to do it (depends on your block), but you'd be way ahead in the you'll-never-guess-where-I've-been-to-lately curve. So if that's important to you, and who doesn't want to be in on the latest things, you must make a plan. Then you're good to go—but only figuratively.

Don't Do Anything Rash!

First, go online and find out when it's the best time to travel down to the ends of the Earth. If you're lucky, it's right now, because you can't possibly go right now (one has to plan these things!), so you'd have a whole year to check on travel arrangements, wardrobe requirements, places to stay.

Are there igloos there or what?

The thing is that you could procrastinate about this one—without guilt—for a good long time, possibly until hell freezes over, and then you wouldn't have to do a thing. No passports required to cross the River Styx.

Meanwhile, Back at the Den

Closer to home, suppose you have a project you know you should do, like fix up the den. If you just don't do it, you're doomed. The den is there, every day, with all those unread books and unplayed CDs staring you in the face, making you painfully aware of your sloth and indecision. This could lead to digression, depression, or worse. But if you have a plan, you're home free.

Hey, renovations cost money! Plans don't.

Make a list of what needs to be done. Ask other people what they do with their old music and paperbacks. Can you even donate this stuff? Look at home décor magazines. Study the pictures of nice rooms and let that soak in. Then get some paint swatches from Benjamin Moore. Such classy colors they have.

Oh! Make a file. That really helps. If you cut out things and shove them into the file, you can easily put off projects like this for years, with just the slightest tinge of guilt. Don't you feel better already?

And now, I have to stop procrastinating about the den, not to mention Antarctica, and finish writing this book. Well, not actually writing it. Thinking about writing it. Wondering about how long it should be. And what the cover should look like. Doing an outline. Coming up with why I can't possibly do it today. Maybe I'll go to that exhibit at the Met after all. If it hasn't closed.

Sounds like a plan.

Nothing Doing!

66 Idle hands make work for the devil. 99

So, if you're busy, like, say, dealing drugs or stealing cell phones, you're on the side of the angels? But if you should, god forbid, just chill out for a while, you're doing something immoral?

I prefer the opposite advice, "Don't do something, just stand there!" Or to paraphrase romance writer Barbara Cartland, never stand when you can lean, never lean when you can sit, and never sit when you can lie. Down, that is. Lying is a sin.

Nothing Doing!

A minute ago, I tripped on the carpet. *Bad* carpet! And if I weren't so naturally graceful and athletic (not), I would have fallen.

And if I had fallen, I might have hurt myself (ouch!), and the rest of the afternoon and maybe the evening or even many days thereafter would have been taken up with dealing with that. I mean, I could have sprained an ankle, or broken one even. I could have sustained bruises, with blood and everything. Just cleaning that up really eats into your day.

Maybe I would have had to go to the (GASP!) Emergency Room. At the very least, I'd have to do something with band-aids, which are never where I think I put them, so that alone would have taken hours.

But I didn't fall. I caught myself, and I dutifully returned to the computer, where I am writing this. You think these things write themselves? But the thing is, I could have had that accident. I almost did, didn't I? And since I didn't, and I saved all that time dealing with the consequences, don't I have some free time coming?

Can't I Just Goof Off for the Rest of the Day?

Hell, yes.

With all the extra time I saved, I feel that I can watch an

old movie, or Dr. Phil or Judge Judy even. Hey! I might learn something. Or listen to music and thumb through all those magazines stacked up on the coffee table. (I never have coffee there. Does anyone? Maybe I should try it today.) I don't even have to actually read anything all the way through, just, you know, browse.

Better yet, I could tap into my inner Italian and do absolutely nothing. Perhaps you've heard the expression, *La dolce far niente.* The sweetness of doing nothing. Not from an American, you haven't. We feel that we have to be busy doing SOMETHING, anything, all the damn time. We feel guilty if we're idle.

When people call and ask me what I'm doing, I sometimes make up things. I would never say, for example, "Oh, I tripped on the rug and nearly fell and could have done god knows what to my person but I didn't so I took the rest of the day off." They wouldn't understand. Funny, but even saying that you're watching a game on TV is more acceptable than admitting you're just goofing off.

And unless we're working, shopping, cooking, cleaning, building something, or discovering the cure for male pattern baldness, we feel that we're doing nothing.

But think about it. Even when you're doing "nothing," and the Italians are the absolute masters of this, you're actually doing tons of things.

You probably got up, at some point, then you had coffee, or some vile protein drink or other, you brushed your teeth, maybe even flossed(!), you watched *Good Morning America*, you did stuff at your computer, you had breakfast, you had lunch, you made a phone call, you made the bed (or just brushed off the crumbs from the crackers you had last night), you got dressed (sweats and a T-shirt count), you washed your face, a little, you looked out the window, you stared at the refrigerator. I could go on and on.

Plus, think of the thinking that sometimes occurs while you're doing "nothing." Answers to questions you've long pondered can come out of nowhere when you're not trying too hard to figure them out. Besides, haven't you ever heard that other great piece of advice, "First, do no harm?" Well, you can't do any harm if you're not doing anything. Right?

So be lazy! Be actively inactive! Be Italian! You know you've always wanted to be. Although these days, most Italians are nearly as busy as we are. They drive like maniacs, so they must have something to do. Or maybe they're just in a hurry to get where they're going so they can do . . . nothing.

Look, just like me, something could have happened to you today that would have taken up hours and hours, maybe the whole day or a large section of your life. But it didn't.

So use this extra time wisely: Do Nothing.

Let me know how that works out for you. If you're not too busy. . . .

Let Them
Eat Worms

66 The early bird catches the worm. **99**

This makes total sense if a) you're a robin and b) you enjoy dining on slimy creatures of the mud.

Yes, yes, I know, this unpalatable platitude is not supposed to be taken literally, and the theory is that if you get up early, you'll accomplish more. True, to a point. But I don't believe it's always the right thing to do. In fact, you'd have to get up pretty early in the morning to prove it to me.

Let Them Eat Worms

Why does everyone get up so damned early?

One of the symbols of wealth back in the day was that you could sleep till noon.

If you were truly blessed, you'd be someone like Bette Davis in *All About Eve*, with a sassy servant (how politically incorrect!) named Gertie who would bring you breakfast in bed, late. Breakfast would probably include a Bloody Mary, hair of the dog and all that, because you were out late the night before doing something terribly glamorous. Then you would read the papers and get ready for (a late) lunch.

Only farmers got up at dawn—because they had to. But when society changed from agrarian to cosmopolitan (or martinian), people started to sleep later and later—because they could. Then the pendulum swung back. With a vengeance.

What happened over the past few decades is a kind of creeping guilt, which makes you feel that you can't sleep in—ever—and that the earlier you get up, the better a person you are. Getting up early may have its benefits, but because we've always been a little-does-good-more-does-better society, we're not thinking straight on this one. Maybe because we're sleep deprived?

I Can Get Up Earlier Than You Can!

Whatever the reason, people are finding more and more ways to let you know how early they get up: 6 AM these days is nothing; you have to say 4 AM to make an impression. 3:30? Why bother to go to bed at all. These people aren't farmers. They get up before the crack of dawn for all sorts of reasons: They commute ridiculously long distances, they have impossibly crammed schedules, they have to go running before work, it's the only time they can walk the dog because their dog has an impossibly crammed schedule too, or some other damn thing.

And they make you feel like a positive slug about sleeping later than they do. Early equals virtue, late equals evil.

I wouldn't mind this so much if I thought that most of these people were actually accomplishing something extra with all this extra time. And some of them are: Dr. Oz probably does more in a day than most of us do in a lifetime.

But it's my observation that most early risers are not human after 9 PM and therefore can't go to or actually enjoy a concert or show, and that they spend a lot of time complaining about how busy (and tired) they are, and are forced (sometimes by illness) to completely collapse from time to time. Some of them fall asleep in their soup (literally) at dinner.

Yes, there are those super-achievers who move mountains on three hours of sleep a night. I've read about those people. But most of us need the good old eight hours, and I, for one, don't believe for a second that you need less as you get older. That might have been true once, when all anyone over fifty was expected to do was sit on a rocker and reminisce about the old days. Not now! We are active and getting more so. We work until a later age, and when we "retire," if we ever do, we travel, exercise, send nasty letters to AARP, join the co-op board, bother our relatives, read silly novels, write a blog. You need a lot of sleep for this.

Eight hours used to be a respectable amount of sleep; ten was sleeping in. A popular book once advised, "Sleep 'till noon and screw 'em all." Was this literal, I wonder? Anyway, back then the general rule was: Never call anyone before 10AM unless you knew for sure that the person was an "early bird." Nowadays, when almost everyone gets up at some ungodly hour, "early bird" means the 4:30 dinner at the diner. I'd rather eat worms . . .

So, if you need eight hours of sleep a night, and you go to an evening event that ends at, say, 11:30, and you get home after midnight, and you fall asleep by 1AM, you have to sleep until 9AM. Do the math. And if the event runs long, or you're wound up and can't get to sleep for a while, you need to sleep even later.

But if you do, someone will call at 7:55, and be totally amazed that they've woken you up. Still asleep? It's nearly 8! Weird. Strange. How very retro. You must be sick. You are morally corrupt. Most important: You totally lose the How Early Can We Possibly Get Up? Contest. And that's what it's all about, I think. Competition. To be the biggest, the best, the richest—and now, the earliest.

Sleepyheads of the World, Unite!

You have nothing to lose but those bags under your eyes! Do something drastic about this godforsaken trend. Be daring, be original, be rested. Unless you actually enjoy those early hours, and while my fevered brain cannot fathom this, I've noticed that some people actually do, figure out the latest time you can get up—not the earliest—and still get the job done.

Sleep late once in a while—without guilt. Be lucid after dinner. Get through a show without falling asleep. Enjoy New Year's Eve next time. And actually listen to the words of *Auld Lang Syne*. Then explain them to me: Am I supposed to forget my old acquaintances, or remember them? I get it that we should all have a drink (if that's what "a cup of kindness" means), and lucky for me I can drink a little something because I sleep really late on New Year's Day.

But if you really must get up so early, every damn day of the year, please stop wearing it like a red-eyed badge of courage. In fact, don't even tell me about it. At least not until after ten.

The 13th Floor

66 Don't be superstitious. 99

Oh, I don't know. Some things, like not walking under a ladder, actually make sense. Others are more questionable. Does stepping on a crack really break your mother's back? Not likely. Still, I've stepped on a lot of cracks, and my mother does have spinal stenosis. Of course, she's 98.

But how about the number 13? Unlucky? Just a silly superstition? Contractors don't think so. Most new buildings skip from 12 to 14 when they number the floors. I used to think, Who are they kidding? But now, I'm not so sure. . . .

The 13th Floor

Every writer has a "bad story" story. This is mine.

Once upon a time, I co-wrote, along with a friend as misguided as I, an unsolicited script for a play. We called it *The 13th Floor*, and since we didn't know what we were doing, the title was probably the best thing about it.

We were young and we needed the money.

The friend who collaborated on this brilliant piece of literature (NOT) and I both had small apartments in the same building.

"How small were they?"

"They were so small, you had to go outside to change your mind." That's an old joke, but trust me, these apartments weren't spacious.

Anyway, we wrote this play for a new show that was trying to bring back radio drama. It didn't work: the show or the play. But miracle of miracles, the producer actually bought our script for the incredible sum of $200 (100 clams each!) for all rights.

All right!

When we heard the news, we whooped and hollered and rolled around on the floor, although you couldn't do all that much rolling on a rug that was more like a bathmat. Still, we were as happy as two unpublished writers who were about to be published could possibly be.

And then (dramatic organ music here) tragedy struck . . .

A few weeks later, those bastards at the network (does that phrase sound familiar to anyone?) withdrew their offer. Just like that, with some flimsy excuse or other. Bankruptcy? Death? An Act of God? No explanation could possibly have satisfied us, nothing could have dulled our pain, and we were too shocked to protest very much.

Things couldn't get any worse for our two heroines but, of course, they did.

Music gets more dramatic.

A few weeks after they told us they weren't buying our story (well, we weren't buying theirs either), we were listening to the show—and we heard a version of our script being broadcast on the air! Our idea! Our script, sorta. Okay, it might have been a better version, edited by more experienced writers— but it was ours! And don't forget, we were young and needed the money!!

Alas, we were too inexperienced in the ways of the world (why didn't we sue?) to fight this thing. We let it go, and as we say these days, moved on, and little by little it faded from our memories. For years, though, we celebrated Veteran's Day together, feeling that we now were survivors of some sort of war.

So, after all this, why am I not bitter?

Simple.

Organ music gets dreamy and upbeat.

To this day, I remember in vivid detail how happy we were to have sold that script. In my mind's eye, I can see that little apartment, the sycamore Tree-That-Grows-in-Brooklyn (even though this was Manhattan) framed in the catty-corner window, the Murphy Kitchen, the little red ratty rug, and especially the whooping and rolling around in pure joy.

On the other hand, I don't even remember any of the bad stuff, the details of how this played out, so to speak. I don't recall for example, if those dastardly bastards even bothered to change the title of the play, or if they had the gall to use that too. Harrumph.

The other day in the elevator of my building, which ironically is just a few blocks away from the brownstone where I lived back then, someone got in on 13, and because I know he's an actor, I told him I had written a play called *The 13th Floor*.

"Good title," he said, and I'm pretty sure that he walked away with a positive impression of my writing talent. I could have told him the truth about the play, but I figured I should quit while I was ahead. Why push my luck?

Men in Skirts

66 Listen to the Experts 99

Well, yes, your accountant can tell you if you can deduct your pantyhose as a legitimate business expense (you can't). Your doctor can warn you to cut back on sugar (you should). Your lawyer can advise you whether or not you can sue your boss for being a jerk (you shouldn't). But when it comes to fashion . . .

Beware of experts bearing advice.

Men in Skirts

Did you hear about the exhibit at the Met Museum in New York called *"Bravehearts: Men in Skirts?"* It portrayed men throughout the ages wearing all manner of skirts—caftans, saris, sarongs, dhotis, and, of course, kilts. In conjunction with the show, many designers and other fashion experts began urging men to be more "fashion forward" by wearing skirts, which, they noted, "free the legs and are less restricting."

Okay, it's a fun idea to imagine hot, young, male models on the runway in skirts. But if you're looking for an actual trend for actual men, don't hold your breath. It will never happen and here's how I know.

The Skirt and I

Sometime last year, I rediscovered my legs. I bought a jacket, as usual, but instead of matching pants, it had a skirt. With a leather strip and a sort of ruffle on the bottom. Cute. So I thought, well, what the hell.

This is not the first skirt I've bought in the last decade, but this time I actually wore it. I loved the experience! I admit it: it made me feel more feminine, and I behaved accordingly: think tilting of the head, tossing of the hair, crossing of the legs. What could be wrong with that?

I'll tell you what. The next time I wanted to wear The Skirt it was raining. Not a drizzle, not a shower, but a downpour, and the arts club I was headed to is a ten-minute walk away. Not only would I get wet, I mean, really wet, I would ruin my shoes. Because, you see, with a skirt, you have to pay attention to what is on your feet. They show.

And so, with a heavy heart—alas, no longer brave—I abandoned all hope of being fashion forward in a skirt and heels, and reached instead for the good old black pants suit and the black waterproof boots. Fashion backward, perhaps. But practical. And as I walked to the club in the rain, I remembered why I stopped wearing skirts in the first place:

It's Too Damn Complicated!

It can be cold. It can be wet. It can be damp. There are drafts!

You also have to consider the condition of your legs: Are they shaved? Bruised? (Mine get battered by running into the opened dishwasher). Do you have stockings that go with the skirt? And OMG, what about the shoes? If the shoes go with tights, then you don't have the shaved, bruised thing to worry about, but tights can be, well, tight. If the shoes show your toes, you need a pedicure.

This is freeing the legs? This is less restricting?

Men in Skirts? I Think Not.

Men are those people who say things like, "But you already have a pair of black shoes." When men ask what to wear, they really mean, "Do I really HAVE to wear a jacket?" They fight getting a new pair of shoes, then decide that the pair you've pushed them into buying is the only pair on Earth they can walk in, and refuse to try on anything else ever again.

Men want it to be easy, comfortable, and brainless. Maybe they're right—and maybe all those fashion experts are wrong about a lot of things.

These "experts," remember, are the people who brought us wasp waists (you had to have ribs removed), the flapper look (you had to bind your breasts), hoop skirts (you couldn't sit down) and 6-inch heels (you couldn't stand up). Men would never stand for (pardon the pun) these styles, and perhaps women shouldn't either. Have we been foolish all these years for listening to the experts and being such willing slaves to fashion?

Because here's the other side to the story: I had a perfectly wonderful evening wearing my trusty old pantsuit. I met a lot of people and talked myself hoarse, agreeing with the bartender that I still have it, although I can't exactly remember what "it" was. I didn't need to wear that skirt, and considering the stormy weather, I'm glad I didn't.

So the next morning, with a slightly sore throat—from talking too much, not from wet legs—I read about the exhibit at the Met and this push to get men to wear skirts. HA! I rasped. HA! It takes far too much effort and creates the distinct possibility of being uncomfortable.

Even if they didn't shave their legs or wear peek-toe sling backs (and wouldn't they be a sight in their new skirts with hairy limbs and worn-out old clodhoppers!), they'd still have to deal with extreme weather conditions and indoor drafts.

But what about women? Does it have to be all pants all the time? Not for me! I've got that skirt and I'm going to wear it. Once in a while. Weather permitting. Some clear warm night, I'll flounce into the arts club with a smile on my face and new, non-deductible pantyhose on my smooth-shaven legs. In the meantime, flounceless but happy, life goes on.

And just in case you were wondering if men in skirts might be less prone to violence, and that it would help them to embrace their feminine sides and not be so eager to start wars and other nastiness—forget it. Think about *Braveheart*. Or the Praetorian Guard. Or African warriors. Or cavemen.

By the way, how many of the male designers and fashion experts who attended the Men in Skirts gala opening do you suppose actually wore a skirt? Zero. Zilch. Nada. Not a single one. Oh, well. Maybe it was cold that night. Or damp. Or raining. Or maybe the experts don't always listen to themselves.

Define Casual

66 Always dress appropriately. **99**

Okay. I'm for that. Except for one thing: What the hell is appropriate these days? Women wear flip-flops to the office and running shoes to the opera, but then, mysteriously, turn up dressed to the nines at some function I was told was "casual."

Poor me. I never seem to get it right. So I ask, for once and for all, someone out there please . . .

Define Casual

It used to be that when you went to a party, there was no such thing as casual. You "dressed up" in the outfit of the moment, complete with matching shoes, purse, and whatever jewelry went with The Look.

There was the A-Line, the Mini, the Little Nothing (AKA the Shift), long full skirts, long tight skirts, short tight skirts, pumps, mules (now called slides, and for good reason), platform shoes, huge hoop earrings, circle pins, simple strands of pearls, and oh, you get the picture.

You had to be up on the current fashion, then cut down on nonessentials, such as food, in order to afford the clothes. Well, you had to fit into the dress anyway. The only other obstacle was getting through the party without someone else showing up in the exact same outfit. Which happened.

To understand this quaint phenomenon, see almost any rerun of *I Love Lucy*. But if Lucy and Ethel had problems then, think of how they'd handle going out for an evening these days.

Fact: There Is No Real "Look."

The reason for this, say the fashion gurus, is so that we all can express ourselves, and not be constrained by the one-style-fits-all straitjacket mentality. Oh really? Could it be that the actual reason is that no one has had the originality to champion an actual style since—when? The eighties?

All right, it was a dreadful style: shoulder pads a linebacker could love, real gold jewelry so huge it looked fake, beige pumps. For a vision of the eighties via Florida via a TV sitcom, watch *The Golden Girls,* where the clothes are so . . . colorful, they take on a life of their own.

But at least the eighties had A Look. As Truman Capote said, bad taste is better than no taste.

Think of a decade and A Look will pop into your mind: the twenties: Julie Andrews in *Thoroughly Modern Millie*, the forties: Barbra Streisand in *The Way We Were*, the fifties: anyone in *American Graffiti.* The sixties had two looks: *Easy Rider* and *Breakfast at Tiffany*'s. Sigh. The seventies had terrible prints and big collars. For some reason, I think of *Sanford and Son.*

What Is the Look Today?

T-shirts? Eileen Fisher? Jeans? On the slippery slope from simple to plain, we started to look like Agnes Gooch in *Auntie Mame*. (Grey cardigan, anyone?) For years, there was a banquet of colors out there being ignored, even ridiculed. Lime green and hot pink are supposed to be making a comeback, but try wearing anything but black in certain circles at your own risk. Except for that exciting year—was it 2010?—when grey was declared the new black.

Who do the clothes of today look good on? My theory: on the truly beautiful because it does nothing to detract from their beauty. And on the very plain, who can look very plain and be very in. The rest of us—the many, many millions yearning to go shopping, buy something nice, look as good as we can, and be more or less in style—are often out of luck.

Mixed-Up and Mismatched

Lucy and Ethel would find today's clothes totally baffling, which, now that I think of it, would make for good comedy. Fashion magazines have always been unintentionally hysterical, telling you that this year's look is "very wearable," while featuring 7-inch stiletto heels and skirts so tight they cut off the circulation to your brain.

Lately the ads in these magazines are funny because nothing goes with anything else. They feature individually beautiful objects that don't belong with each other. Every season, someone declares something is in, but it's a thing unto itself, not a piece of the whole. Example: One year it was Burberry Plaid. Then it was camouflage gear. Did any of that coordinate with the flimsy shoes in pastel fabrics? This year, or was it last year (?) argyle was back, but for sleeves only. I think.

We are expected to mix and match, be daring, create our own look. It works (most of the time) for Carrie on *Sex and the City*, but not for too many of the rest of us.

There Are Exceptions

Some women have no problem with all this. They have perfect pitch when it comes to clothes, and have style rather than fashion. They do create their own Look. Others just ignore the whole thing and look dowdy/businesslike/ethnic/whatever.

Some are young and gorgeous and look outstanding in anything that shows their navels. Some are movie stars and get to look drop-dead gorgeous, at least once a year at the Oscars.

But frankly, most women don't look as good as most women used to look. This wouldn't be a bad thing if nobody cared, if women were using all that Lucy-Ethel energy to do something fun or find a cure for cancer. But women still care—a lot—about appearance or there wouldn't be a billion-dollar cosmetic industry and all these TV makeovers. And men still care, because bless their little hearts, they are and always will be visually oriented and don't get around to noticing your soul until later. Much later.

One New Year's Eve long ago, I borrowed an original Balenciaga outfit, and still remember the way that gown and coordinating coat made me feel. We dressed up then.

On a New Year's Eve in this millennium, you'll probably be told that the party is casual. Sigh. What the hell does that mean? To me, casual is what I'm wearing right now: a hoodie, drawstring pants, and socks. But I am obviously mistaken. One party I went to was supposed to be casual, a kind of clam bake at a beachfront house, so I wore white capris (AKA clamdiggers) and a nice tee. Most of the women were in little silk or satin dresses with spaghetti straps and Manolo Blahnik slides.

I Didn't Get the Memo!

I'm beginning to wonder if there's a club I don't belong to that demystifies "casual" for any given event. Please put me on the list: I am very confused!

I saw a movie called *The Anniversary Party* that takes place in LA, where everyone came in different degrees of casual/cool/structured/unstructured/ratty/elegant. One guest, a frazzled new mother, buzzed out on various and sundry drugs (those sundries will really get you), changed her clothes halfway through the movie, from a nondescript shirt and loose-fitting pants to a Jean Harlow white satin gown. Nobody seemed to notice, that's how cool they all were. As for the men, some were in suits, some shirtless in shorts. To me, these people didn't look like they were at the same party.

All this casualness was very, very calculated. The credits for the movie had a long list of designers, and I have to assume that the jeans that Gwyneth Paltrow was oh-so-casually wearing were not from the Gap. She looked great, but she fits into the young, beautiful (slim and tall) category and the less we say about her the better.

And if anyone thinks that looking like you don't care how you look is easy to achieve, they need to see Robert Altman's film *Ready to Wear*. A young photojournalist stands in front of the mirror, trying on dozens of combinations of ratty-looking clothes so that she can achieve just the right touch of grunge, which she eventually does.

Even the Guys Are Confused. A Little.

Life is easier for men in the fashion world. Quick! What did Ricky and Fred wear? Who cares. But choosing what to wear is not without its problems even for the boys. Going to dinner used to mean a jacket and tie. Then a jacket. Now, who knows.

It's . . . casual! The men wearing jackets look better, but they are often pissed off because they see others who look more comfortable.

I have given so much bad advice to my husband that I roll my eyes and say nothing when he asks me whether or not to wear a jacket. I usually have no idea, except for the opera (I insist) and our arts club (they insist). This is so refreshing and makes life much simpler.

The worst is an invitation that says "Black Tie Optional." I hate that! Talk about wishy-washy, noncommittal, not taking responsibility. Black Tie or not—make up your mind! I once went to a Maybe-It's-Black-Tie-Maybe-It-Isn't evening in East Hampton and people showed up in all forms of dress including shorts and sneakers. The only men wearing tuxes were the ushers, and they were complaining.

The beauty of Black Tie for men is that once you get a tux, it's really easy. There are no decisions, and it looks marvelous, darling. For women, formal is more complicated, of course. At the very least, it involves a lot of preparation, including manicures, pedicures, hairdos, and makeup. And it might mean getting a whole new outfit with shoes that go with the look and can actually be walked in, at least from your apartment to the cab, or house to the car.

For formal occasions, women are supposed to look well-groomed at the very least and glamorous if possible. It's a bit of trouble, sure, but if the invitation says Formal or Black Tie, at least you know where you stand.

Besides, it could be worse. The affair could be . . . casual.

With a Thong in My Heart

66 Beauty is in the eye of
the beholder. **99**

*Sure. But what if the beholder is you, and you're beholding
yourself in the 3-way mirror of a harshly bright dressing
room as you're trying on bathing suits? It's not a pretty
picture. . . .*

With a Thong in My Heart

Buying a bathing suit.

Somehow, I feel that I don't have to say another word. And yet, of course, I will.

The fact is, no matter how colorful the suits are, and it's alleged that they will be colorful this year, buying a bathing suit will give you the blues.

Here are some adjectives that come springingly to mind:

Dreaded, humiliating, humbling (not exactly the same as humiliating), life-negating, tiring, stressful.

Please feel free to join in!

And then there are the nouns:

Disaster, failure, disappointment, compromise, defeat.

There are sentences, too:

I came, I tried, I wept.

I came, I saw myself in the 3-way mirror, I fled.

I came, I saw a lot of suits, none of them fit.

The people who design bathing suits for women are sadists. Every year, they decide that a certain style or cut is in, and you're stuck with it whether it fits or not.

It never fits.

Last year, it was the halter-top. If you're flat on top, it just lies there, looking useless. If you're big, you hang out. You want to hang out on the beach, not out of your bathing suit. I hate halters.

For a while, the bottoms were being cut higher and higher, higher and higher, higher and higher. This was supposed to "elongate the leg." What it did was show more cellulite. Now, bottoms are cut a bit higher, and some suits even have ruffles on the bottom. Do you remember the pictures in the children's books of elephants in tutus? If you try one of these on you surely will.

The people who run the bathing suit departments are also sadists. There are so many suits, you can't believe there isn't ONE that will work. There isn't one.

But nevertheless, you take 20 or 30 into the dressing room. One lives in hope.

The people who design dressing rooms are the worst kind of sadists. The lighting makes everything (and I mean everything) look hideous.

Then, just when you thought that it couldn't get any worse, it could, and it will.

If the top fits, the bottom doesn't.

If the cut is good, the color isn't.

If the style is nice, they don't have your size.

I hate men. Actually, I can abide them every now and then (most of the time, really), but not when shopping for a bathing suit. Men have three style choices: short, medium, long. (Speedos are pretty much out—except for that weird guy on *Real Housewives of New York*.) Most colors come in most sizes. And they are IN ORDER OF SIZE! Women must scrounge around desperately seeking sizes.

One good thing: they invented the tankini. I like these, because they're cooler (literally and figuratively) than one-piece suits, and it's much more convenient when you have to go to the bathroom. Also, when you're lying in the sun, in a prone position where things don't hang out quite so much, you can raise the bottom of the top (is that clear?) and get some sun on your midriff. Remember, when all else fails, tanned flab looks better than pale flab.

Unfortunately, the latest trend is having the tops and bottoms of bikinis and tankinis sold as "separates," which get, well, separated, and when you've finally found the perfect ("perfect" may be too strong a word here) top, you can't find the bottom that goes with it.

Oh, well. We always like to put a positive spin on even the most dire situation. So here's one: Last year, I bought a cute top from Michael Kors on sale at Saks that goes with the black bottom from one of last year's suits. I did it! And it was a bargain!

Okay, that may not work for you.

Besides, you need a spin of your own. So try these on for size:

- I never liked the beach anyway.

- The mountains are so much nicer this time of year.

- He loves me for my mind.

- Thank god, the cover-ups are cute this season

Or my very favorite reason for not getting all bitter about this:

The eyes of anyone who happens to "behold" you at this point will be blinded by the sun, if not your beauty, and won't even notice what you're wearing.

And then there's this cheerful thought: You won't have to shop for another bathing suit for another whole year.

Alien Vibrators from Hell

66 Embrace change! 99

Which nobody likes to do. Unfortunately, you are constantly forced to make changes—even in your sex life, presuming you have one.

The next story is for all of us, with or without partners, married, single, involved, involved with ourselves, whatever. It's about something that wasn't working, and I did, indeed, have to make a change. But I must warn you that it contains some graphic images, even though it was written a few years ago when I was quite naïve in the ways of sex toys. I now know that almost all vibrators are large, colorful, and shaped like dildos. But at the time, I was looking for something a little more basic. . . .

Alien Vibrators from Hell

They say that as you get older, new trends begin to seem "alien" to you. Not necessarily good or bad, just strange.

Take cars: sexy once mean sleek and low like a Jaguar, but the new hot thing in driving machines is the huge Hummer Limo. Sure seems alien to me.

But talking of hot, sexy—and big—let me tell you about my latest adventure in the Pleasure Chest, a sex shop in Greenwich Village, where a tall, dark, and handsome stranger and I discussed vibrators. Well, Old Reliable broke, or as Samantha said on *Sex and the City*, "It made this pathetic little sound and died." When the clerk suggested that she probably had worn it out, she said it wouldn't be the first time.

But I, alas, I am no Samantha, just one of those ladies shopping for a little something to put in her goodie drawer. I wished I had Samantha there to give me advice, as she helped someone on the show. "Not that one, honey, too many bells and whistles. And that one will burn off your clit." Even with panties on, the woman wanted to know? Even with ski pants, Samantha assured her, with great authority.

No Matter What They Say, Size Matters.

Well, this clerk was no Samantha either, although, as noted above, cute enough. He showed me their most popular brand, a huge dildo thing in hot pink with some sort of attachment that I don't even want to think about. Gulp! My last vibrator had been a discreet little device and I just wanted to replace it. But the clerk looked blank when I described it, and I began to realize that he was probably about three when I got that old, obviously outdated model. And that all the vibrators in the store looked like dildos. And that I was hyperventilating.

The clerk probably noticed how uncomfortable I was (it was hard to miss) and showed me the one smaller model they kept in stock, a clever little battery-operated gizmo called the Pocket Rocket. So without further ado, I bought a Pocket Rocket of my very own and got out of the Pleasure Chest as fast as I could.

And guess what—the Rocket rocks! Plus, it's great for traveling. I sincerely hope that this means I won't have to go back to the Pleasure Chest and face that daunting array of huge plastic dicks ever again. I just found out about a new place, owned by women just for women, and I'll definitely go there. Someday. But I have a sinking feeling that women or no women, the choices will be no different, and I will be awash in a sea of multi-colored organs from another planet.

I'm thinking I should buy a half dozen Rockets, so that when they become obsolete, I won't have to visit a new, improved alien sex shop of the future where the vibrators will look like I can't imagine what. Maybe by that time, Orgasmatrons (introduced in the movie *Sleeper)* will be part of all upscale Manhattan apartments. I can see the ad in *The New York Times* classified now:

CUM SEE YR DRM APT NYC: 2BR, RV VU, WBFK, EIK, O-TRON.

Some aliens, apparently, do come in peace.

Keep the X in Xmas, Shall We?

Every year I have to come up with identical gifts for my husband's four grown-up daughters. Something fun, but not too expensive. In 20 years, I've gotten them gifts like the pleated goddess scarves from the Metropolitan Museum, key cases from Ferragamo's in Venice, change purses from the Judith Leiber warehouse sale, and other assorted goodies, but over time, it's gotten to be a bigger challenge.

You know what I'm thinking, so tell me: is this idea too alien? Do I dare? Should I go from assorted goodies to sordid goodies? Should I give them something they really can use?

Well, it would be interesting unwrapping the presents under the tree. Very educational, especially for the grandchildren. Or maybe not. They were probably expecting the large hot pink dildos and will think that the little Rockets are quaint.

By the way, it's said that things *should* begin to feel alien as you get older so that eventually you'll be ready to leave the party—and the planet—that is, be more prepared for death. Could be. As you may know, the French—oh those Frenchies!—call the orgasm a "little death."

It is not known, by me at least, what they call a dildo. Dildeau, perhaps? And are theirs more fashionable than ours? And do they use them a lot? Hey, no judgment. Whatever works.

But maybe it's time to get off this subject . . . and move on to the next platitude.

Existentialism at the Cheapie Nail Salon

66 Keep up with the times. 99

Very important. You don't want to be thought of as a dino-saur, do you?

Quick! Can you even imagine what life was like in the Olden Days, before computers and smart phones, texting and tweeting? The times we live in will go down as the dawning of The Age of Technology (maybe there'll even be a song and a play with full frontal nudity), and in many ways, that's a good thing. But sometimes, just sometimes, don't you wish we were back in the Age of Aquarius, with the tie-dyes and bell-bottoms, and without all these devices that rule our lives?

Existentialism at the Cheapie Nail Salon

Today I had my nails done and looked into the meaning of life.

At the same time!

This is through the miracle of modern technology, specifically the iPhone, which I discovered is much better than old copies of *People* when my hands are trapped under the nail dryer, a bit of technology I have my doubts about. Does it really matter if you use it rather than just wait 15 minutes?

That is a question not even Soren Kierkegaard, who I was looking up on my iPhone, could answer. Although, being a philosopher, Soren would certainly have given it some serious thought.

But why was I looking up Kierkegaard in the first place? I can't remember. It must have had something to do with something. Everything does, after all. But what? Maybe I was trying to improve my mind while getting my chipped toenails repaired. Maybe I was bored. Okay—the real reason? Because I can.

With a smart phone in hand, you can look up anything. A quick review of recent searches reveals some of the things I get Googly-eyed over.

Sol Alensky: Who was he and why is Newt Gingrich so obsessed with him? I had to find out. Answer:

Community organizer, liberal, definitely not Newt's cup of tea, or whatever amphibians drink.

How many feature movies have ever been made? Just curious. And there is no answer.

IMDB (Internet Movie Database) They don't know either.

Infomercials: I was asked to give a testimonial, but didn't learn anything to help me figure out what to say. Will have to wing it.

Fifty Shades of Grey: Known as Mommy Porn. I'm not a mommy, but all I can say is Holy Crap!

Never On Sunday: Just saw this film, which I loved long ago, and found it to be pretty ridiculous this time around.

Medea: The Greek tragedy that Melina Mercouri loves to see in the aforementioned movie: where she changes the horrific ending, including four murders, to "And then they all went to the seashore," a line I've used more than once myself.

The artist called Hundertwasser: Trying to find out if the litho I have is worth anything. It is, actually, although it's not a litho, but a color etching, and it's called *Be Careful When You Walk on the Prairie*. I thought it depicted a sailboat. That's how much I know about art.

Patnyc.com: A link to my blog. Just checking.

Diphtheria: Diphtheria? I think this had something to do with *Downton Abbey*. Or maybe it was *Boardwalk Empire*.

The Magnolia Organic Spa: They're having a sale on facials, but who has the time? I barely got to the nail place.

Tippecanoe and Tyler Too: It turns out that this has nothing to do with overturning a small boat, but was a popular campaign song extolling the virtues of William Harrison, a hero of a battle at Tippecanoe, wherever that was, and his running mate, John Tyler. Who knew.

And that's just today. At the Cheapie Nail Salon.

So. Is this a good thing . . .

Or not?

Well, I now know what Tippecanoe is about (and so do you), although how that will affect our lives remains to be seen. Maybe it will give us perspective on the current state of our political campaigns. Maybe not.

But my head, and yours too, is crammed with not exactly useless, but not all that useful, information. And you have to wonder whether all this searching for facts keeps us from actually thinking about important things, like what to have for dinner.

Or even figuring out how all these places, which we New Yorkers affectionately call the Cheapie Nail Salons, started springing up on every block in the city, offering manicures and pedicures at prices so low you simply can't afford not to use them. Now they've become institutes of higher learning. Or at least, higher trivia.

And by the way, who was Kierkegaard, anyway? A nineteenth century Danish philosopher, who is considered the first existentialist, whatever that means. I used to know. Something about "existence precedes essence," whatever that means. I see another Google search coming. I think I got distracted by the Tippecanoe stuff, but in my relentless search for meaning, I really need to know these answers, although I have already forgotten the questions. At least I'll never be bored.

Wait a minute—wasn't Kierkegaard the one who said:

"Boredom is the root of all evil."?

Quick! Where's my iPhone? I have to look that up.

Life by Lottery

66 You make your own luck. **99**

Luckily, it's also true that "80% of success is just show-ing up." The problem is that in today's world it's getting increasingly harder to succeed—to achieve The American Dream (or even 80% of it)—even if you do show up, study diligently, work long and hard, and generally do the right thing.

Some of us think that from now on "making your own luck" will involve buying a lottery ticket.

Life by Lottery

They Wuz Robbed!

Just before April Fool's Day a few years ago, thousands of people in Brooklyn thought they had won *The Daily News* lottery—which would have paid them $100,000 each—only to find out that the numbers were wrong because of a printing error. Ouch!

The lawyer representing some of these non-winners (it would be cruel to call them losers) sez it ain't about the money, see—it's about "the loss of a dream." The *New* American Dream—the dream to win the lottery.

Requiem for a Dream?

My take on all this is that the gulf between the haves and the have littles, which is growing exponentially as we speak, has become so enormous that winning the lottery is the only way some of us can ever make it. Since the *Old* American Dream, which involves hard work and thrift, is being downsized every day anyway, wouldn't it be so much easier to forget all that drudgery and penny-pinching and simply have the money handed to us in one nice big fat lump sum? While we're still young enough to enjoy it?

Fortunately for those who feel this way, the actual lottery is not the only way to hit the jackpot. A jury I was on awarded three million dollars to a cop injured by a fall on the job, leading one jury member to wonder if the only way she could ever have enough money to get by was to get hurt and then make someone pay. It could be an accident of any kind, some sort of medical malpractice, or even a really, really hot cup of coffee.

Okay, okay, I don't want to make light of pain and suffering (and I have it on good authority that the woman in the coffee incident, AKA the McDonald's Coffee Case, actually was scalded), but doesn't it seem to you that things are seriously out of whack?

Consider this: If you fall down and break your arm in the forest (where nobody hears it fracture), all you get for your trouble is a cast for people to write their initials on. But have the same accident at the right place at the right time, and you can sue for hundreds of thousands. Millions, even. This gives new meaning to the term "lucky break."

The Great Cosmic Lottery in the Sky

Let's face it, life always has been a lottery, beginning with the accident of your birth. Were you born rich or good looking? Both? Neither? Are you smart at least? Your parents might have been nurturing or abusive. Did they have the decency to leave you an inheritance?

You're dealt a hand by the Fickle Finger of Fate, and sure, it depends on how you play your cards, but most people can't bluff well enough to win the pot unless they are holding at least three aces, maybe four. If you don't begin with a head start (like inheriting a huge fortune), you may never catch up, and in fact, you will probably keep falling further and further behind—either in reality, or in relation to where you think you should be. As Alice found out in Wonderland, you have to run really fast to stay in the same place.

Falling into the Gap

Why is this happening? Two reasons. First, there's that pesky ever-widening difference in wealth. The masses toil away to get by. One state, which shall remain nameless, has a minimum wage of $5.15. Really! I just looked it up on line. Another site calculates that Mark Zuckerberg makes $8800 a minute.

Although not quite that rich, lots of people are earning multiple millions each and every year, and that can add up to real money. We've always had the rich, and the super rich, who, it's true, are very different from you and me. But there's more of them than ever. There's a lot of money out there. Look at it this way: if you had been making 10 million a year for the last 10 years, even if you spent money like it was going out of style (and it is!), you'd have a fair amount left over.

Not long ago, alongside articles on the editorial page of *The New York Times* lamenting the sad state of the economy, was a huge ad for an "extraordinary" diamond necklace, a huge piece of jewelry that looked as if it was worth more than the combined net worth of several emerging nations. And there must be enough people out there with enough cash to buy this thing or the advertiser wouldn't find it worthwhile to run the ad.

So, with their numbers increasing (more and more of the

rich with more and more money), more and more stuff has to be put out there to feed their jaded palates—things that tempt those who can't afford any of it. And it's not just high-end brands like Fendi and Ferrari, although both these brands are beyond the reach of most of us. (Okay, there are fake Fendis, but you can't fake a Ferrari.) It's an increasing number of things you think you *have* to have, just to get by. Even if you shop at Walmart or Best Buy, all this really adds up.

Ever notice that when you announce you've bought a new Sony flat screen TV, an iPhone, iPad, or an iWhatever-TheyComeUpWithNext, or announce that you are taking an expensive vacation to Barbados, or getting a facial at a fancy spa, someone says "good for you." Is it really? We have been conditioned to think that we deserve all these toys and all that pampering, and maybe we do. But it sure costs. Add that to the high price of even the bare necessities, and it's easy to back yourself into a corner where there seems to be only one way out: win the lottery.

Here in the City That Never Cheaps, it will cost you $2000 a month to rent a space the size of a walk-in closet, and you'll have to shell out a million simoleons to buy an "average" apartment. Of course, you might already have a rent-controlled place. Or bought a place when the market was soft. But isn't that just another form of winning the lottery?

The big one last week was 210 million. And ten lucky people won it! Of course, 21 mil is pocket change to more and more of the "1%" these days, but to most of us it would be the ultimate American Dream. It would certainly make up for that original, totally unfair turn of events, whereby the Great Cosmic Lottery in the Sky didn't make us billionaires in the first place. The nerve!

But what if we play and we don't even win. I hate to tell you this, people, but the odds are against us. Could we trip and fall on the way home from the newsstand on a hard-to-see but dreadfully dangerous protrusion in the sidewalk, obviously caused by the extreme and willful negligence of the City of New York, and sue for $21 million? $41 million? A billion: Why think small?

Can we get a really, really good lawyer? Can we win the case? Are we rich yet? Who knows. Maybe we should hedge our bets and buy yet another lottery ticket, a winning one this time. We should only be so lucky.

What's with "The Weight?"

66 Learn a foreign language to improve your mind. **99**

Does that include the words of popular songs? I don't know about you, but I am capable of loving a song without having the slightest idea of what it is actually saying. So how about we try, together, to improve our collective minds by translating this one. . . .

What's with "The Weight?"

Nobody doesn't like "The Weight," that great song by The Band —you know, the one that starts out, "I pulled into Nazareth" and gets more confusing with every word. I was amazed to find out that it's only #41 on the *Rolling Stone* Greatest Songs of All Time list: it's on my Top Ten.

Of course, I have no idea what it means.

But after reading all that advice about learning new things, and since I already do crossword puzzles, I decided to do something meaningful with my life: Google the song and uncover the true meaning of "The Weight."

So here goes:

I pulled into Nazareth, I was feelin' about half past dead;
I just need some place where I can lay my head.
"Hey, mister, can you tell me where a man might find a
bed?"
He just grinned and shook my hand, and "No!" was all
he said.

Are you with me so far? I figured that Nazareth was Biblical, didn't you? But according to Wikipedia, it's a town in Pennsylvania. Go figure. Anyway, it's clear that the traveler is looking for a place to stay and the guy he meets can't or won't help. "Half-past dead." Brilliant. We get that.

And then we come to the famous chorus . . .

Take a load off Fannie, take a load for free;
Take a load off Fannie, And (and) (and) you can put the
load right on me.

Okay, for starters, I always thought (and others still do) that it was Manny, not Fannie, but that's a minor detail. I also assumed that "take a load " was a hit off a joint (hey, this was The Band), but the most popular interpretation seems to be: you help me out, I'll help you out. Whatever. Anyway, now the plot thickens:

I picked up my bag, I went lookin' for a place to hide;
When I saw Carmen and the Devil walkin' side by side.
I said, "Hey, Carmen, come on, let's go downtown."
She said, "I gotta go, but m'friend can stick around."

Okay. Who the hell is Carmen? The Devil I know, which is better than the Devil I don't know, but is Carmen telling the traveler to go to hell, or what?

And then we get to meet yet more characters: Miss Moses (Miss *Carmen* Moses—or are they two different people?) and Luke (this must be Biblical!), plus our new BFF, Anna Lee.

Go down, Miss Moses, there's nothin' you can say
It's just ol' Luke, and Luke's waitin' on the Judgement
Day.

"Well, Luke, my friend, what about young Anna Lee?"
He said, "Do me a favor, son, woncha stay an' keep Anna
Lee company?"

After the chorus (Fannie or Manny again), there's yet another name:

Crazy Chester followed me, and he caught me in the fog.
He said, "I will fix your rags, if you'll take Jack, my dog."
I said, "Wait a minute, Chester, you know I'm a peaceful
man."
He said, "That's okay, boy, won't you feed him when you
can."

Ho boy, now we got Chester (wasn't he in *Gunsmoke*?) and
his dog, Jack—and have to decipher that cryptic exchange between him and the traveler. Rags? Peace? Feed the dog? Say
what?

And then:

Catch a Cannonball, now, t'take me down the line
My bag is sinkin' low and I do believe it's time.
To get back to Miss Annie, you know she's the only one.
Who sent me here with her regards for everyone.

Miss Annie? Fannie? Manny? Anna Lee? Crazy Chester?
Jack? Luke? Carmen? Miss Moses? Have there ever been this
many names in a single song? I am so confused.

So Let's Ask Lead Songwriter
Robbie Robertson. He Should Know, Right?

Robbie says that the song was inspired by the surrealistic films of Buñuel and that it deals with the impossibility of sainthood.

Well, that certainly clears things up, doesn't it?

But wait. Mr. R also says that the song is also about the difficulty of doing something simple, like saying hello to someone (regards from Miss Annie) while passing through a new town—without getting yourself into an "incredible predicament." Okay, if you say so.

Others say all sorts of things: The Weight is the burden we all feel to deflect sin and become more . . . saintlike. Really? We do? Or, that it refers to the afterlife, where the traveler lays down the burdens of the world. Or a place between life and death. Or a hooker named Fanny. Or a hooker's fanny. Or the clap. AIDS. The South. The Civil War. The Sixties. Life Itself. Nothing at all. Maybe you have to be stoned.

I know, I know. You're not supposed to take the lyrics so seriously: it's only rock 'n' roll and, you love it—so don't analyze it to death. Which has been done on the Internet, trust me. And yes, it's entirely possible that no one, not even The Band, or maybe especially The Band, really knows what it all means.

But you can't blame a girl for trying to learn something new and improve her mind. Maybe I should just take up Chinese. Or mahjongg.

Princess and Proud of It

66 Be a good sport! 99

In other words, "DON'T be a princess."

Nonsense! It's important—no, crucial—for you and for all your loved ones—that you learn to be a true princess. If you are surprised by this statement, a) you are not already a princess and b) you really need to read the following. It could change your life. I'd stake my royal crown on it.

Princess and Proud of It

Yes, a princess is fussy, needs frequent manicures, likes cute cocktail napkins, and never, ever takes the first seat she's offered in a restaurant.

But a true princess is also the one who leads the charge (usually metaphorically) when her kingdom is in peril. Look at it this way: A princess takes care of her peeps. In style.

Never Leave Home without a Princess

Let's say you have to spend a few days in the hospital or go for one of those fun medical tests where you need a companion. Sorry, but it happens. In these cases, always, repeat *always*, choose a princess.

A princess will make sure everyone is paying attention to you and will not be pushed around by anyone in authority. She's a princess—neither man nor bureaucrat can possibly intimidate her. She's also good at getting a cab or a car to get you home in comfort. (She probably won't drive, but will hold your hand.) She'll make sure that your meal is more or less edible and that you get that extra juice you ordered. She'll get you a blanket if you're cold or more pain meds if you need them.

She doesn't like to be hungry, cold, in pain, or inconvenienced, and she'll figure out the easiest, least esthetically-challenged way to make sure you aren't, either.

On the other hand, the absolute *worst* possible person to help you out in situations like these is a true stoic. This grin-and-bear-it type will simply, well, grin and bear it, because that's what this sort does. A little pain, a long wait, a meal from hell: would this person make a fuss? No way. The princess? Way. All the way.

On a White Horse Even

How do I know all this? I'm proud to say that a boyfriend in days of yore once called me a princess, and before I could strangle him with a nearby boa or bop him on the head with my professional-weight hair dryer, he explained the concept I've been telling you about today.

He was in the hospital recovering from some injury or other (they're all so tedious, aren't they?), and the light over his bed was broken. He was a serious reader; this was a serious problem. So I set out to find a lamp, determined to beg, borrow, steal, or do whatever it took to get it. A Princess does what a Princess has to do.

Tried everything. Talked to the nurses, the head nurse, the orderlies, the maintenance department, the radiology department (something to do with light, right?), the police guards on the first floor, anyone who'd listen. No luck. But finally, I got to the top. I spotted the perfect lamp in the office of the CEO and somehow, mainly by wearing down the guy's secretary by repeating the phrase, "You don't understand" over and over like a velvet cudgel, I got the thing out of that office and into my boyfriend's room.

After that, even though he knew that I could barely tell one end of a horse from the other, he always pictured me as the Princess on the White Horse charging forth to defend the kingdom. I liked that image.

What you need to remember is that it's always an advantage to have a princess around. She likes nice things, so her place will be tastefully decorated, and she'll fix up yours if you let her. She looks good, she smells good, and if she buys you a tie or a bathing suit, it will not embarrass you. She'll take you (or get you to take her) to nice places. Contrary to popular belief, she usually can cook, because she likes to eat well and can't always, like you know, go to a restaurant.

Sure, she can be high maintenance. But she's worth it.

A true princess, wanting the best for herself, also wants the best for you, and you can bet your royal ascot, she'll get it. If you're lucky enough to be in her kingdom, she'll take care of you in the manner to which she thinks you should be accustomed. Worse things can happen to a person.

Don't Get Mad—
Get Nasty

66 Be Nice. **99**
Variation:
66 It doesn't cost anything
to be nice. **99**

Oh yeah? What if it cost you a lot—such as your mental health? Medical science hasn't quite caught on to this theory, but remember, they had a hard time giving up leeches and bloodletting and believing in germs. One of these days, you'll be reading about how being too nice is bad for you in **People** *or* **Us,** *let alone* **JAMA.** *But for now, you'll have to take my word for it.*

Don't Get Mad—Get Nasty

You know how you always hear that the man who went berserk and shot his wife and dog was "such a nice guy." And the mailman who went postal was "always so helpful" and "never got angry." Well, they'll never be able to say that about me. Or you, if you're smart.

Let's face it—you're always a little ticked off at someone. That loudmouthed woman on the bus talking incessantly on her cell about nothing, *nothing!* That idiot in your office who never gets anything right *but still has a job*. That asshole on the highway who has *the nerve* to cut you off.

It's Not Nice to Be So Nice

Are you going to take this sitting down? You shouldn't, you know. It's a well-known scientific fact, or will be, that it's important to do small but nasty things on a regular basis to get even for all the maddening things people do to annoy you.

If you don't, the ill feelings build up and up, and at some point you'll do something really bad. Left unchecked, this situation could be . . . fatal.

Random Acts of Nastiness

Just little things. The trick is that the nastiness has to be minor, yet satisfying.

Let's say that the loud lady on the bus finally reaches her stop and leaves her newspaper —better yet, her groceries or (if she's really been intolerable) her briefcase. You see what's happening, and you could call out. But why? Say nothing. Mind your own business. It's not your job. Sure, it's nasty, but isn't that the point?

This also works when you find something in the copy machine and don't return it to that guy who does everything wrong—this being yet another proof of that. Hey, he never gets fired anyway, so leaving the document in the copier where others may see it—or (do you dare?) throwing it away—will only cause a little temporary inconvenience.

On the other hand, you probably shouldn't do anything about the asshole on the road, except to express your road rage at the highest possible decibel. It would be great if he ended up with a flat tire and you could drive on by, smiling. Or suppose he asked for directions and you knew the way, and you also knew a really, really long, very indirect route and . . . . But these are merely pipedreams. There are lives involved here, so the asshole in the car usually just gets away with it.

Name-Calling Is Good for the Soul

By the way, "asshole" *is* the technical term for anyone committing an offense against you in a moving vehicle. With off-the-road offenders you can be more creative in your name-calling: besides idiot, there's always moron (not politically correct, but satisfying, and not quite as offensive as retard), cretin, nincompoop (old-fashioned, but it'll get their attention), lamebrain, birdbrain, shit-for-brains. Ever notice how many expressions contain the word shit? I also feel compelled to point out that any of the above expressions can be prefaced by total, absolute, or, of course, the ever-popular f-word.

Muttering names under your breath is a start, but not nearly fulfilling enough. You have to actually do something:

Nasty Bits

• Send someone who's bugging you an e-mail warning that it must be forwarded to 47.5 of his dearest friends in the next 10 seconds or his favorite organ will fall off (make sure he's not a musician, or this won't work) and he'll have terminal flatulence (this works for anyone).

• Leave gum under your seat at the theatre. Broadway prices could make you cranky enough to do worse. Legitimate theatre gets more points than movie houses, where everyone is a slob anyway.

• If you're feeling generally fed-up and need some quick emotional relief, put something in the wrong recycle bin. Oh, I know, I know: the planet, the plague of plastic, the environment, civic duty, blah, blah, blah. But you don't do it all the time, so you won't destroy the Earth just this once. Besides, there is considerable evidence that everything ends up in one place anyway.

• You know that nosy neighbor down the hall? Open a piece of junk mail that gets into your mailbox by mistake then slip it under his door. It won't do any real harm, I mean who cares that he gets the Valued Customer issue of the Victoria's Secret catalog, but it will make him wonder what else you've seen. And know.

• How about those irritating forms in the doctor's office? Especially when you've answered those damn things before. What if you filled it out correctly . . . except for one little thing? One guy I know checked 'yes' for the "Are You Pregnant" box, another gave his sex as "Reptile."

Nastiness Is Its Own Reward

These are just a few examples. Be creative and come up with your own nasty bits. I know you can do it, and believe me, it will make you feel SO much better. If done properly, it will not hurt anyone in any meaningful way, and will not get you slapped, arrested, fired, or suspended from your bowling team. It doesn't cost anything, has no calories, nobody ever has to know—and it's good for your mental health.

Remember: the serial killer you save may be . . . you!

TMI: Or, Is Privacy Dead?

66 Knowledge is power. **99**

Yes, that's true. It is important to know things. Certain things. Important things. But not every damn thing. And not every damn thing about every damn person. If I sound cranky, it's because I am. Like everyone else, I am bombarded with all kinds of information. And there are lots of things I'd rather not know.

TMI: Or, Is Privacy Dead?

You have to ask?

With a few clicks on Google or Bing, you can find out almost anything about almost anyone. If you want to dig deeper, it will cost you a few bucks, but if you really care, you'll cough up the dough.

Isn't it amazing just how much dirt we all seem to crave? And of course, the media loves giving it to us. True, if you're a celebrity, you give up privacy. But how much is too much? Even before ghoulish media coverage of events like Michael Jackson's death, and Princess Diana's life (and death), I realized that privacy was dead. For everyone.

It was back in the nineties, when the Pope's colon surgery was reported by the media in excruciating detail. There was even a diagram of his intestines in *The New York Times*. Sorry, folks, but that was TMI! People! We're talking about a very private orifice of the Holy Father.

I knew then that nothing was sacred (literally), and since that time, things have only gotten worse.

Yeah, sure, some of this information is good: Katie Couric let us watch her very own colonoscopy and that inspired many people to get tested. (Note: The words "inspired" and "colonoscopy" are not usually found in the same sentence. In my inner circle, we have other words for this procedure.) But honestly, I don't have to hear about everyone's colonoscopy, celebs and non-celebs alike. It's bad enough that I have to get these things myself; I wish that people would respect their own privacy and not tell me all the delightful details of theirs.

Not When I'm Eating!

Have you noticed the way people insist on telling you things you really don't want to know, usually involving some bodily function or other, during dinner? Your kid threw up? How many times? It looked like what? You found what stuff in your handkerchief? Your panties? Stop! And also: Desist! I want my meal to be happy, or at least mildly pleasant, so at least wait until after dessert.

What happened to "Don't Ask, Don't Tell?"

Okay, so it didn't work for the military. But keep this in mind: You don't have to answer every question, and you should never volunteer certain information.

About age: Let's make a deal. You tell me how much you weigh, and I'll tell you how old I am.

Frankly, I don't care how much you weigh—or how old you are—but this challenge usually works.

People are really sensitive about their weight. And if we don't watch out, your weight—along with your age, your address, your phone number, and the state of your bank balance—will be (GASP!) posted all over the Internet.

Maybe it already is! And people will start talking about it openly.

"Gee, she looks good for her weight."

"He works at Target, and he's, oh, about 240."

"Jim in Human Resources? That pig? He must be in his mid 300s by now."

Don't laugh. We are in the (Too Much) Information Age. Anything can happen.

I know I just told you about TMI, but a) who says I have to be consistent and 2) there's no way to discuss the state of medicine in America today with going into details. Gory details. Do read the next piece anyway, but wait until after dinner. . . .

The Genie Is Out
of the Orifice

66 An ounce of prevention is worth a pound of cure. 99

Oh yeah? But is it worth a pound of flesh?

Could too much preventive medicine add up to a lot of anxiety, discomfort, depression, money, inconvenience—and all that interminable waiting, waiting, waiting. I may just be overreacting because my beloved gastroenterologist (What? You don't have one of these?) just informed me that I am due for yet another colonoscopy. Oh, joy.

Yes, yes, I know. Medical science is wonderful. These checkups and procedures save lives. Mine even. But am I the only one who thinks that all this has gone just a little too far? Are some of us getting too much medical attention? Seeing too many doctors? Getting too many tests?

The Genie Is Out of the Orifice

I arrived at the doctor's office bright and early one morning for a colonoscopy. In the so-aptly-named waiting room, I talked to a woman who was getting her very own colonoscopy for the first time, and was very nervous. I told her not to worry. The procedure is easy: you're in La-La land when they do it. It's the prep part that's shitty, you should pardon the expression, and she had already survived that.

Like many women I know, I have this test done regularly, along with a lot of other preventative procedures. Here's a delightful stroll through one year in the life of an average woman of a certain age—who's not even sick!

First, the Lady Parts

Back in the stirrups again: This year will bring at least two trips to your friendly neighborhood gynecologist, including the ever-popular internal exam and Pap smear. Warning: this visit could lead to a minimum of three more procedures:

This wand is not magic: The first is a pelvic sonogram where someone puts cold, gloppy goo over your stomach and takes pictures of your insides. Then they shove a wand up your vagina to complete the test. Although none of this actually hurts, it's nobody's idea of a good time. You probably won't want to date the technician.

Ouch! Then it's time to get the old mammos grammed—the way they press them down CANNOT be good for you or me. Or them. Sigh. But if you have mammos, you need to get them grammed.

Dem Bones: At 50, you start getting your bone density tested. This is my favorite procedure because there is no "prep" (euphemism for shitting your brains out) and it is entirely painless.

Back to Basics

Open Wide and Say Aah. Next, an annual checkup with your primary care doctor (remember when that one was the only kind?), which used to mean an hour or so of being poked and prodded, and now is all this and more. An electrocardiogram (easy) and a test for lung capacity (depressing if you find out you are substandard in this department), and, invariably, recommendations for more tests and/or a referral to yet another specialist.

Annus Medicalus

So to sum it up, all this amounts to a minimum, on a good year, of one or more trips to the internist, two to the gynecologist, two or three to the gastroenterologist, three or four to various imaging facilities for sonograms, mammograms, and grams of all nations.

Your gynecologist might send you to a urologist if you're getting a lot of urinary tract infections, and if you have acid reflux, your gastroenterologist may insist on an endoscopy to check out your esophagus. If you get dizzy (possibly from all these tests), you may have to see a neurologist. If your feet or knees hurt, you'll be advised to see a chiropodist or an orthopedist.

If you're having stomach problems, you may get to have a lower G.I. test, which involves drinking about a barrel of a delightful barium-laced liquid that tastes like a metal milkshake. Yummy.

In previous years, in addition to most or all of the above I personally have had X-rays, cat scans, and a test to determine if I had picked up parasites in my travels. This test involved feces: let's not even go there.

Sigh. There Is No Going Back.

The nervous lady in the office this morning spoke wistfully of a "very intelligent" friend of hers who doesn't go to any doctors at all, gets no tests, presumably takes no prescription medicines, and gets away with all of it. We both wondered if that woman isn't right. I keep thinking about my sister-in-law's reaction when she first heard what a colonoscopy was. Her exact words were, "You're going to put what, where? I think not."

But here's the problem: The genie is definitely out of the orifice.

Once you get on the medical treadmill, you can't get off.

When you have something pointed out to you as a potential problem, it's hard to ignore the advice and refuse to go to the specialist or take the test. How can you go against modern medical science? What if your doctor is right?

Harrumph. Maybe so, but I have the feeling that all this testing is out of control. My dad died at 99 ½ but who's counting, and my mom is okay at 98. They always took good care of their health but never had most of these hi-tech tests.

On the Other Hand . . .

Did you all get the e-mail about Gilda Radner's Disease, a cancer of the ovaries that can be detected by a simple blood test that doctors rarely prescribe?

Hey, this is one test that doesn't involve a single orifice! I'm asking my doctor to do it immediately. Better safe than sorry, I always say.

Fireworks Rn't Us

66 Keep the spark in your love life. **99**

Okay, I get that. Maybe some sexy underwear. A candlelit dinner. A spontaneous encounter. A weekend in the country.

But, one time, I may have taken the word "spark" a little too literally. . . .

Fireworks Rn't Us

If there are no fireworks in your relationship, you're in trouble.

I was in trouble.

The guy I eventually married and I—the key word here, folks, is "eventually"—were about to have our first Fourth of July together. And yes, that is SUCH a girly thing to say. But I take these things seriously and I wanted there to be, well, fireworks!

Macy's has a great display every 4th of July in New York City, and I heard that the River Café would be the perfect place for viewing them. So even though it was kind of last minute, I called to make a reservation for dinner. Wow! I got it! A table for two by the window! This must be a sign of good things to come, hopefully involving fireworks, I thought. Then thought no more about it, until the evening of the fourth.

The River Café is romantic and beautiful, set just under the Brooklyn Bridge. The only problem, I imagined, was getting there from Manhattan. We could have taken the subway, but I thought that would kill the mood. Besides, I have what is known as Kab Karma: I can get a taxi just about any time, any place, any weather. Not that night.

When we finally got one, the highway had more traffic

than the 60% Off Sale Rack at Macy's (I feel I owe them a plug here), and even though we had left early, we were lucky to arrive before dark. But we did. Phew! A few sips of a very dry martini, stirred not shaken, and some nice piano music later, I casually asked the waiter where was the best place to see the fireworks. He rewarded me with one of those looks I have come to know only too well in the course of my life: *What the hell is this woman talking about . . . ?*

The Wrong Place at the Right Time

After a few minutes of panic, we found out the cold, clear truth: you could go outside, stand on a milk carton, crane your neck, and sort of see the fireworks. But this was NOT the best restaurant for that purpose. That would be the *Water Club* on East 30th Street. In Manhattan. Not far from where we live, on East 22nd Street.

Water Club? River Café? Anyone could make that mistake, right? Oh, never mind.

So anyway, determined to make the best of it, we headed outside at 9:30, where we stood on milk cartons, craned our necks, and sort of saw the fireworks. They probably were spectacular, but who could tell. My chiropractor was the only one who profited from this experience.

Coming home, we decided to take the subway, which was hot and crowded, then we missed our stop and had to walk the rest of the way. When we finally got to our building, the doorman asked us how we were doing (don't ask) and wondered why we hadn't been up on the roof watching the fireworks with the rest of the tenants.

They were great (the fireworks, not the tenants), according to José. José couldn't see them either, because he was stationed at the desk. He, at least, had a logical reason for not going up to the roof that night. Our apartment is on the 14th floor, so it would have been a really short commute. We could have seen the stars, and it wouldn't have cost the moon. Talk about feeling like an idiot.

I wish that I could tell you that we never had any problems with fireworks ever again, but that's not entirely accurate. Every year, something seemed to happen. We froze our asses off on the beach in East Hampton a few times, where you could hardly see the fireworks because of the fog. Several years it rained. Once there were thunderstorms. A few times we were on the Jersey Shore, the beach, not the show, and saw local fireworks. Nice, but not spectacular.

Finalmente. . .

And then it happened! Finally. By some amazing piece of pyrotechnic providence, we ended up in Venice on July 15, for the Festa del Redentore. That's a holiday celebrating the end of the plague in 1576 (like they really know on exactly what DAY it ended?), and, as if the Italians need an excuse for anything, it's a really good opportunity for extraordinary fireworks. *Molto fantastico!*

Truly, they were the best I've ever seen, better than Macy's even, and my (by then) husband got a fantastic photo that was the hit of his one-man photography show.

So our story has a happy ending after all—and a moral even:

"Stick around long enough and there'll be fireworks in your life."

Or at least a good photo op.

Nothing Is Simple:
The Wedding
Bell Blues

66 Keep it simple. 99

So let's say, in spite of all the odds against it, you find a guy. A keeper. Your friends give him a 9.9 (no one is perfect), and best of all: he wants to get married—and so do you. You both agree that you don't want one of those fancy weddings, just something sweet and intimate. And special, of course.

Go ahead and get married: I recommend it heartily. But it is not without a twinge, a smidgen, a not-enough-to-stop you-but-just-enough-to-mention-it bit of bitterness, the nasty news that the wedding will NOT be easy. . . .

Nothing Is Simple:
The Wedding Bell Blues

I recently got an e-mail entitled, The ABCs of Living Well. There was a nifty piece of advice for every letter of the alphabet, especially S, which asked us to "seek simplicity." Oh yeah? What if you seek it, search for it (desperately, even) only to find out the awful truth: Seek all you want, my lovelies, nothing is simple. Especially weddings.

I got married a few years ago after living with my guy for 19 years. Why did I wait so long? I wasn't afraid of getting married. Hey, I really knew this man—you met him in *My Night at the Pussy Cat Lounge* on page 5. But I was afraid of the . . . wedding.

Be Afraid, Be Very Afraid.

In a time when you are expected to have what is basically a coronation, including an engagement party, a rehearsal party, bachelor (and bachelorette) parties, and an after-the-wedding breakfast, I got hives just thinking about it.

You're also supposed to have at least 100 guests, be registered at Tiffany's (or at least, Bed, Bath & Beyond), buy expensive presents for each other, have the best wedding dress ever seen on this or any other continent, and orchestrate an affair that rivals the royal wedding of Princess Diana. And, may she rest in peace, we know how well that turned out.

But before I had a chance to become The Runaway Bride, a miracle occurred: I got a great dress! Not a white, full-length gown (What do I look like, the virgin bride?), but a fabulous silvery outfit—first shot out of the box at Lord & Taylor department store. With coupons! And free alterations! This had to be an omen that everything else would go along just as easily.

As You May Have Guessed, They Didn't . . .

This wedding was going to be a small, intimate affair at the apartment of my very good friend. Perfect! We'd get a terrific caterer and lots of champagne. My two buddies and I would write some of our almost-famous song parodies to perform for the assembled not-so-massive masses.

Still, I, being the bride and all (the groom was cute but oblivious), had to make endless decisions: the guest list, the menu, the *hors d'oeuvres* (all I knew was that I didn't want pigs in the blanket), the servers, the table arrangements, the flowers, and on and on and on. My friend was a huge help, but still. My To-Do List was updated daily and my "W THING" file was the size of the U.S. tax code. I started to feel like Pat of the Thousand Details, and I am lousy at details.

And yet I was determined to keep this wedding simple. It was going to be 35 people, family and a few very close friends. My only really fervent desire was that we have a piano and that we'd perform parody songs written especially for the wedding.

Simple, Right? Weren't You Listening? Nothing Is simple!

First of all, I invited a few too many people (I couldn't help myself), then couldn't get a real count because some of them were out of town and didn't know if they could make it. Many e-mails and phone calls ensued, plus fevered talks with the caterer who had to have an accurate number. In the end, we had a few more people that we should have, but it was basically okay.

Then there was the wedding cake. In my naiveté, I thought a wedding cake was a wedding cake. You know, the ones with lots of layers and white icing and decorations and stuff. But oh, no. There were yet more decisions: dimension, number of tiers, butter cream or fondant, white cake or yellow (white is prettier, yellow tastes better), and so it went. I ordered butter cream with two layers, then had second thoughts (better about the cake than the marriage) that it wouldn't be big enough (also better about the cake), and changed the order. I worried about it up until the actual wedding when a) it was fine and b) I had had enough champagne not to care.

A Few More Little Snags

The shoes. Perhaps you know the heartbreak of wearing a difficult-to-find shoe size. You out there with small or large feet, narrow or wide widths know what I'm talking about. Mine is a 6½ narrow, and they are practically extinct. So I had the dress, I had the pearls, I even had the right bra: all I needed were the shoes. (There's a song in there somewhere.)

And so the search began. I won't bore you with all the details, but let me say that I spoke to shoe designer Stewart Weitzman personally, and now know on a first name basis all the guys at Eneslow Custom Shoes, who rebuilt the pair of gorgeous silver mesh pumps from Weitzman that were, alas, a half size too big and slipped off my feet. A half dozen visits to Eneslow and $125 later, I had a pair of shoes I could bear (barely) to put on, but that would have to qualify as instruments of torture.

I got a pair of silver sandals to change into after the pictures, but honestly, they weren't all that comfortable either. And the expensive silvery stockings bagged at the ankles. Thank god I did a dress rehearsal (literally: I tried on the dress and accessories) in time to get another pair (and a spare) of grayish ones that weren't as perfect, but fit. Interestingly, in my one actual nightmare during all this, I dreamt that my pantyhose fell down during the ceremony. After the wedding, I ended up using the silver mesh shoes as bookends.

And Lots of Songs

What's a wedding without music? At least our song-writing sessions were going great. The two performers and I would meet in my apartment, drink wine, and try to be brilliant. I ran around singing, "I'm getting married in November," to myself of course, and we came up with some great parodies, like "Let's Do It" (Let's Tie the Knot), some fun ethnic stuff (Hava-Nice Wedding, anyone?), including our very own version of *Luna Mezzo Mare*, which you might remember from

The Godfather. It's the one with the chorus "Oh Mamma, Piscia Fritta Baccala, which means "Oh Mama, fried fish." No one seems to understand the significance of this, but it's fun to sing. I created a sing-along song booklet with a photo of the wedding from that movie with our heads superimposed as the bride and groom.

But tragedy nearly struck when the piano player I had hired refused to play on the electric piano in the apartment, therefore creating a mad scramble to rent a bigger one. Which cost a fortune. My reaction was "I want to rent it, not buy it," but I was worn down enough to cough up the dough, when at the last minute I heard about Davie Lewis, a real pro who not only could "play on anything," but could play (and sing) anything. Disaster averted.

The show we presented at the wedding was a huge success. And a big surprise to the guests: Who does parody songs at a wedding? I even got my cousin, who Tony Bennett has called the best white blues singer of today, to do a few numbers for us.

Alert the Media

And then there was *The New York Times*. All through this whole thing, people kept giving me suggestions of What I Should Do. Most of them I ignored. But getting an announcement in the *Times?* Well, that could be fun.

Let me tell you this: If you decide to have a wedding—even after reading all this—and you really want that announcement, make sure you're prepared to sign away your firstborn and to send in a mountain of paperwork at least six weeks before the event. It was, mercifully, way too late, and my contact at the *Times* had moved on, and so I was spared the effort of getting all this together, including a photo of the bride and groom with "the eyes at the same level." I'm not making this up.

And about photos: I asked, begged actually, people not to bring cameras, or at least not to take a lot of pictures. A friend who's really good at it agreed to be the official photographer, and my brother, an almost-famous cinematographer (*Gossip Girl*, for one thing) took movies. But meanwhile, flashbulbs were going off everywhere. Is it only me, or does anyone else think that 10 or 12 photographers for a group of less than 50 is too much? Oh, well, I got to have my Bridezilla moment and made faces at one of the cameras, photos of which were sent out via the Internet before I could protest. (Shades of *Gossip Girl!*) I realized then that I really must Seek Serenity. Is there a 12-step program for brides? There should be!

But that's a quibble. As you may have guessed, the wedding was a triumph. Even the judge was funny: When we asked him to finish up quicker, he said that he only cut it short at a bris. And don't get me wrong, the ceremony was touching as well. I was glad I had sprung for the waterproof mascara.

Comments from the guests include: "Wowee!" "Swanky and fun," "Best show in town!" (Of course, there was a strike on Broadway at the time, so we were the only show in town, but a good review is a good review), "Better than any of my weddings" (and he should know), "Cool" (a teenager), "Not boring" (another teenager). These last two are raves.

I did it, and I'm glad, and I'll never do it again. It's that simple.

Yo, Universe!

66 You can do anything. 99

Sure you can.

Nobody, other than Forrest Gump or the woman in Bellevue who thinks she is the lost Princess Anastasia, totally buys this one. And yet, you hear it all the time.

Yes, you'd like to believe you could do anything. Have anything. Be anything. And there are lots of self-help gurus out there who'd like to assist you in your quest for perfection. For a more-than-modest fee, of course. Most of these positive thinking ideas have been around for years, centuries even, and may have been in early cave drawings for all we know, but all this positive thinking does have its limits. . . .

Yo, Universe!

What good is a "secret" that's been out for thousands of years?

Well, if it's news to you, it could change your life.

The Secret, which had everyone buzzing on Oprah a few years ago, is that everything in the universe is connected—including thoughts—so that what you think directly affects what happens to you. In other words, you get what you ask the universe to give you.

Wow. This is not praying or begging, but like placing an order in a catalog. That Great Cosmic Catalog in the Sky. You have to be specific (size, color, quantity, please), and you have to work towards your goal. But if you follow this advice, you will always get what you want.

Trust me, folks, this is nothing new. I'm not saying it's bad, nor am I mocking it as some did. Maureen Dowd called it a cross between Dr. Phil and the Da Vinci Code. Well, yeah, a little around the edges. If I were bitter, I'd say that it's simply a new way to make money from an old idea. All I know is that when I went to the web site, it asked for $4.95 to enter, and when I didn't pay up, that colorful whirling ball came up and wouldn't stop until I shut down the computer and rebooted. Coincidence? Retribution? You decide.

Anyway, this whole philosophy goes back to the time of

Aristotle (a lot of good it did him!) or maybe even to some cheery caveman who hadn't seen those heartbreaking Geico ads and thought that he could do anything.

Hello? Positive Thinking?

As in: *The Power of*? As in: Norman Vincent Peale? It's no *secret* that he preached these ideas and had a huge following last century.

How about the practice in the early 1900s, revived in the sixties (what wasn't?) of repeating to yourself: "Every day in every way I am getting better and better."

I suppose you could substitute "richer and richer." Or "thinner and thinner." On an episode of *Upstairs Downstairs*, a woman repeats, "Every day in every way my baby is getting more and more male." Hmm. How do you say that in Chinese? Never mind.

I have used a visualization technique called Psycho Cybernetics, from the book published in 1960. The idea is that if you can picture yourself doing something, say, executing a perfect swan dive off the high platform—really picture it, in clear and vivid detail—you can do it in actuality. I know for certain that this works. I, for one, cannot *begin* to imagine executing a perfect swan dive anytime in this lifetime. And sure enough, I can't.

All right, that's not fair. I have successfully used visualization to win over difficult clients, get the apartment I wanted (you think that's easy in Manhattan?), ride a horse (not well, but without falling off), even find a man!

Yes, yes, I swear it's true. I worked with a counselor nearly

20 years ago to focus on what I really wanted. So I pictured myself and this person, whoever he was, cooking together and laughing. Soon after, I totally got my wish. It came with a few features I didn't imagine (let's not go there), but really, although we do bicker about how much salt to put in the pasta water, we have a happy relationship. This positive thinking stuff really works!

It's always been true that like attracts like. So if you're happy—or depressed—that's the kind of person who'll gravitate towards you. It's also true that *How a Man Thinketh* (a book written in the 1890s by James Allen) really does count. It counteth a lot, according to Allen:

"All that a man achieves and all that he fails to achieve is the direct result of his own thoughts."

The book calls this idea "The Strangest Secret."

Ever hear of Dennis Waitley, Tony Robbins, or Wayne "You'll-See-It-When-You-Believe-It" Dyer? They're all in on "The Secret" and will be happy to share their version of it with you. Check Amazon for books, tapes, books on tapes, and anything else you can think of.

I haven't read *Think and Get Rich*, but I suspect the title says it all. And what about *Chicken Soup for the Soul*? Isn't that another way of saying all this? For a *condensed* version (I couldn't help myself) here's what Loretta Lynn told me about overcoming obstacles when I was interviewing her for a book on her early life: "Honey, I didn't think about what I didn't have, but what I did have." Worked for her, didn't it?

I used to tell people to "talk to the universe" to solve their problems. They hated me for that. People don't want to hear that they may be the cause of their own troubles, and that they could have a better life if they gave themselves an attitude adjustment. If you tell them this too aggressively, they may be tempted to give you one, upside the head.

Look on the bright side! Now you know The Secret. You can be rich. And thin. And find love. And never grow old. Well, maybe not that, but you can't have everything. Although if you follow this Secret stuff to its illogical conclusion, you should be able to achieve eternal life, if that's what you want.

Never mind! We'll ask Oprah (wherever she is) about that later. Meanwhile, let us go forth in our newfound wonderfulness and unleash the glorious power of our thoughts into the bountiful universe.

Negativity? Don't even think about it!

She Lived a Full Life

\-

66 Write your own eulogy. **99**

Actually the advice was, "Write your own epitaph." You're supposed to do this so you'll think about what is important in your life and live each day accordingly. I liked the idea of writing an epitaph but went even further (what a surprise): I wrote my own eulogy, using the platitudes you always hear at funerals and memorial services. It struck me as funny that you can't get away from them—even at the end.

She Lived a Full Life

If someone is reading this, then we know why we're gathered here together. Frankly, Pat would have preferred a wedding or a bar mitzvah, but they weren't options. So, she prepared a boilerplate speech for her own demise encompassing all of the usual platitudes and clichés so that no one else has to do it. God forbid, she should be a burden on anyone.

Platitude Numero Uno (The Mother Of All Platitudes): "She lived a full life."

Well, yes, she did. Of course, that depends on what you mean by "full," as in full of what? Do four husbands count? That kept her hands full, so to speak. Then there were the engagements, some broken, which raise the ever-popular question: Engaged in what? There was even a broken heart or two, which she claimed enabled her to understand the words of country western songs. Besides, being in love is an altered state, and Pat liked altered states. Being a little buzzed, riding in a car at night, listening to Willie Nelson. How bad could that be?

Perhaps this love of altered states stemmed from the fact that she was petite, and from an early age had to have everything altered. Sleeves, hems, waistbands. You name it. And the damn pockets were never in the right place anyway.

The altered states of her youth included a little weed, no big thing in the universal scheme of things. Later, under extreme duress, like, you know, surgery or something, she favored Demerol. Ah, yes. And as time went by, she turned to martinis, and unlike some *people* who shall remain *nameless*, they never let her down.

Pat traveled a lot, especially in Italy, and finally got to Venice when she was 50 with Lou, the Love of Her Life. Funny, how she was still 50 a number of years later at her annual 50th Happy Birthday Party. Well, CleoPATra was ageless, too. Get it: PAT? Cleo-PAT-ra? A few of you are laughing. Very few. Explain it to the others. Thank you.

Pat was intellectually curious and always full of questions. That contributed to her success with Mega Books, where she was president and founder and sometimes caught mice in the back office. Not to mention catching staff smoking pot. She announced that day that if she wasn't smoking, nobody was, and that was the end of that.

And yet, even to the end, there were some questions she could never answer. Like how the hell the publishing industry ever got anything done when what they wanted was "something new and different that had stood the test of time." Or why the coupon you keep in your wallet always expires the day before you finally remember to use it. And where did those knots in the cord on the hairdryer come from. Don't you have to *tie* knots? What's that about? And let's not even get into the chin hairs.

She did come to understand certain things. Like how there

could be a "one-day" sale at Sleepy's *every single day*. What she found out, after a lot of investigation (and you have to say this about her, she was tenacious), was that every day one single thing is on sale, so that literally, there is a one-day sale, every day. So much for truth in advertising. But honestly, she didn't buy their claim on the TV ad that "There's no other feeling like it in the world—the excitement, the thrill, of getting the perfect mattress at the perfect price!" That was someone's idea of the greatest feeling in the world?

Well, that person certainly hadn't lived a full life.

Platitude #2: "At least she didn't suffer." OR "She's not suffering any more."

Pat was hoping very much for option #1, but it's safe to say one or the other.

Platitude #3: "She kept a clean house."

Or at least not a dirty house.

Okay, so the towels weren't hung perfectly.

And there were all those Junk Drawers from Hell.

And the dust ruffle that hid a multitude of sins.

Hey, it was clean enough, let's move on! This platitude sucks anyway. Who was she, Martha Stewart?

Platitude #4: "She will be missed."

Hopefully, yes, by her friends and family, you who are gathered here together. But also by Atlas Dry Cleaners, Stuart Weitzman shoes (What will the man do with all those size 6 1/2 narrows?), the Gramercy Fish Market, the French Butcher, Amazon.com, the CVS pharmacy on Third and 22nd, the Metropolitan Opera, and the doormen at Gramercy House. She was a pain sometimes, but a good tipper.

Platitude #5: (Although she could be cranky . . .) "She had a good sense of humor."

For example, because she had a lifetime of insomnia, she requested these words on her tombstone:

WHEN I SAID I WANTED A GOOD NIGHT'S SLEEP . . .

THIS IS *NOT* WHAT I HAD IN MIND.

People who didn't get the irony (poor dears) thought that this was too negative so she changed it to:

FINALLY, A GOOD NIGHT'S SLEEP . . .

Later, when she decided she didn't want to be buried and would rather be cremated (There's really no good option, is there?), she figured that the short version would work better on the urn anyway. Less engraving.

Platitude # 6: "She was always good for a laugh."

This is not the same as having a good sense of humor.

For example: she had a habit of losing things. Not funny, you say. How about her skirt on Park Avenue? Actually, Pat didn't think that this incident was particularly funny, or even noteworthy: it was a wraparound skirt, and she had a lot on her mind. Hey, it could happen to anybody. She also lost her underwear in Rome, but that's another story. (See: Oh! You're Supposed to Throw *Coins*! on page 45.)

Platitude #7: "She was generous—to a fault."

For one thing, she was always willing to share her best recipes. She had three: deviled eggs, meatloaf, and she could never remember the third—but it, too, would probably give her cardiologist heart palpitations. The secret to the meatloaf, which now can be told, was rye bread. Actually, she gave the complete, detailed recipe to many people, knowing full well that they would not follow the directions exactly and that her status as Supreme Meatloaf Queen would be safe forever.

Pat liked short speeches, so enough with the platitudes and clichés. Just a few other things:

Don't send flowers: she had allergies. Pool the money and have a cocktail party at the apartment. If it's winter, light a fire. And open the windows: the place is always overheated. But it has great light.

Pat liked light. There is always that possibility that she is, indeed, going to the light, but nobody really knows for sure, do they. Anyway, at the party there should be deviled eggs, meatloaf, and triple crème cheese (no recipe required). Hell, she doesn't have to worry about the cholesterol anymore, and neither should you.

And then she wants you all to go forth and have a great dinner, maybe at Gramercy Tavern—but make a reservation or you'll never get in. Before dinner, she suggests a very dry

Martini, straight up, stirred not shaken, made with Belvedere.

If you need a toast (Do we have to do everything for you?), drink to the fact that she never lost her hourglass figure, even though, as she was the first to point out, that as time went on, the sand had definitely shifted.

Still, she'd drink to that, and so should you. And, whatever you do, do not forget the extra olives.

Note: This eulogy is unedited and not ready to go—but then, neither was Pat.

Some Final Thoughts. . .

So. Did you learn anything?
More important: Did you laugh?
And did you figure out that you—
and everyone else in the universe—
has something to be bitter about.
But where's the fun in that?
Much better to relax, bend the rules,
and see where that takes you.

If you want more of this wit and wisdom,
because contrary to popular belief
too much of a good thing is
just about enough, go to my blog:
I CAN'T BELIEVE I'M NOT BITTER.

You can access it at
www.patnyc.com
Or at **www.i-cant-believe-im-not-bitter.com**.

Acknowledgements

Thanks to my editor, Susan Lurie, for pulling it all together, Diana Giuseppone for her advice (I asked for it!) and for being my best friend and biggest blog fan, Marc Nadel for his inspired caricature and for saying things like "sophisticated and clever" about my writing, Greg Wozney for the design of this book and for putting up with all the AA's, Steven Freivogel for his technical help on the blog, and for dragging me, kicking and screaming, into the world of social networking.

About The Author

Author, editor, publisher, and blogger, Pat Fortunato writes the humor blog, I Can't Believe I'm Not Bitter, which you can access at patnyc.com. She lives in New York City with her husband, Lou, a lot of books, and many things she can't find.